EAST OF THE SUN

A NEARLY-STONED WALK DOWN THE ROAD IN A DIFFERENT LAND

SIDDHARTHA SARMA

TRANQUEBAR PRESS
An imprint of westland ltd

61, 2nd Floor, Silverline Building, Alapakkam Main Road, Maduravoyal, Chennai 600095
93, 1st floor, Sham Lal Road, Daryaganj, New Delhi 110002

First published in TRANQUEBAR by westland ltd 2010

ISBN 978-93-80658-36-0

Typeset in Goudy Old Style by SÜRYA, New Delhi

TRANQUEBAR PRESS
EAST OF THE SUN

Siddhartha Sarma is a journalist based in Delhi, and an author. His debut novel *The Grasshopper's Run*, and a non-fiction book, *103 Journeys, Travels, Trips and Stuff*, have been shortlisted for the 2009 Crossword Children's Book Award. He is also an occasional budget-traveller, and is known for exaggerating his experiences and drinking much tea on the road.

NOTE FROM THE AUTHOR

This is not a tourist guide. If you're packing up for the parts I have described, this will not substitute for one of those multi-coloured touristy thingies you see which have nice little maps with black dots on them and squiggly rail tracks all over with names and phone numbers of hotels.

If you wish to travel in the North-east, you need to be humungously well-informed about the parts you intend to reach in case you don't have a local contact to show you around and host you, be prepared for an occasional absence of amenities, and always keep in mind this land is different from other places you might have been to. (And if amenities matter so much on the road perhaps it is better to stay home, eh?)

What you will read here is a series of observations and, I guess, anecdotes, as well as numerous facts which I refuse to acknowledge as factual or otherwise, so if you go by them and mess up, it's entirely your fault and don't blame me. But I, awesome as I am, take all the credit in advance if you happen to be there and discover things for yourself which will help you look at the world in a slightly different way. For the North-east is a place best visited as a traveller, not as a tourist. Yep, there's a vast difference between the two.

But do visit.

ONE

Hey, peoples. Bet you've been wondering where I've disappeared to. At least, I hope you have. I haven't kept in touch as much as I would like to have, because most of the parts I have been in do not have much in the line of cellphone networks or the Internet, but I try my best to keep you folks updated.

I've been on the narrow road. Tell you all about it.

So this morning, about a month ago (maybe it was longer than that or shorter, I'm a little fuzzy about details) and I was at work, full of beans, as the expression goes. I opened the mailbox on my terminal. Don't ask me what was in the mailbox, probably nothing important.

Then I closed it. I had to leave. I had to get out. So, I left.

There are some days. Bet you have them all the time. You wake up in the morning, brush your teeth, look forward to the rest of the day stretching on and on, and somewhere among the morning rituals you realise there's a snatch of a song or something looping around in your head. Sometimes it's a song, but the worst mornings it's some arbit ad jingle. Don't you get them?

I take these days in a light-hearted spirit. That is, if it is not an arbit ad jingle, I refrain from tearing my hair out. No problem, I say. It happens. Confucius say: 'True master not bother by ad jingle', etc.

Ed.: Great. A 'Confucius say' joke and the story is yet to begin. This is going to be one of those books . . .

And then, once in a fair while, I wake up and pay real attention, because that's when Tolkien's *The Road Goes Ever On and On* is looping around my cranium. Not the one which goes 'The road goes ever on and on . . .' (I can see a lot of hands raised at the back there, but you got it wrong. Ha! So you thought just because Ian McKellan's Gandalf sang it in *The Fellowship of the Ring* it was the only road poem in the Legendarium? Double Ha!). Not so, *mesdames et messieurs*, but far otherwise:

> *Still round the corner there may wait*
> *A new road or a secret gate,*
> *And though I oft have passed them by,*
> *A day shall come at last when I*
> *Will take the secret paths that run*
> *West of the Moon, East of the Sun.*

Lovely stuff, isn't it? But then, all of Tolkien is marvellous. Okay, okay, I can hear some of my long-suffering friends groaning about Tolkien already. I'll take it easy. Promise.

Ed.: Yes. Please.

Anyhow, beautiful, haunting poem and it's a bit of an alarm clock. You see, for the last decade or so, if I ever hear that song l. around my c., I have to get on the road. It's Pavlovian, what can I say.

As things stand, I hear it about twice a year, following which I set off on a run. I suppose it's a function of my growing older (I won't say 'growing up' because that might be open, I suspect, to some debate), but these days that poem goes around for a few weeks inside my head before I take some steps, or a lot of them, as it were.

There are several ways to travel. You can get one of those package deals which might or might not cut costs, depending on which agent you're using and how much of the travel plan and things you can cross-verify. But hey, if you could do that you'd make a plan yourself, wouldn't you? So getting an agent means someone else deciding how much you are going to bring back when you set out.

Journalists are strung along another line, which is a bit addictive and, comforting, yes, that's a word you can use here. We have PR or companies or organisations fix junkets on which we are invited and feted to the degree of our seniority, news value hidden deftly within the junket or the capacity of the organiser. While that might fetch another pin on the map of places you've been to, you do not really get to learn jack about the land, the people, everything that makes it what it is. I have had to revisit some of these places solely because they were too delicious to just be there and back with what we call a double-column story.

What else? Ahh, yes, the third way is to make your own plan and travel. If you are very particular about mod-cons and such, the availability of these will, naturally, be the first criterion when you choose a location or a route. You know: a certain kind of hotel, some types and levels of transport. That would be what I call the wide road. However, there might be a few places in India where the wide road does not reach, and until it does, you are missing something.

So you pack light, take whatever transport you can get, stay wherever you can under whatever reasonable conditions, eat whatever is available, optimise your travel schedule so you are on the road mostly at night when you can sleep and get the whole day to see things, stop complaining if things get a little sticky and use the golden rule: when in doubt, improvise.

The idea, then, is to travel light and quick, through the Brahmaputra Valley to East, or Upper Assam. From there, I zook down to where the Naga Hills begin, journey to Kohima, and onward, through those hills, into the Imphal Valley.

After this impressive feat, I shall continue south through Manipur and eastward into the southern Patkai Range, finally crossing into Myanmar.

I have done parts of these areas before. You know, the kind where you set up a forward camp, make a run, return, make another run. This time, I'll be on the road from start to finish, regardless of the weather, the road, the food or whatever else is going on in those exciting places. Never a dull moment on that road, let me assure you. Minimum provisions, maximum entertainment.

That, in short, is the narrow road, and that's the best way to travel.

There are a few policy decisions I make for this run. Some of these are long-standing rules, arising from avoidable experience. Some others are new.

I never travel with people I don't know very well, or have met recently. This is a practical rule. We meet a lot of people in the normal course of things, and some of them tend to make a lot of claims about this and that. Particularly about travelling. There seems to be something about travel that makes random people break out in all kinds of patently phony and, worse, unverifiable accounts. Hearing them, one might think half the mountaineers, deep sea divers, adventurers and intrepid explorers have been lurking around us and we didn't even know about it. Golly.

So we set out with them, and the first thing we know, we are in the lurch. Two instances come to mind.

About four years ago, two of my friends and I decided to go to this tiny place called Chitkul in Kinnaur district in Himachal. We had good reviews of that place and had been told we better go there quick before it was swamped by awful Potato-Chips Tourists (more about this insufferable species later). Ah, so you've been there. Excellent.

Now, along comes this other chap, whom my friends knew better than I did. He wanted to come along. He even volunteered his car. He scoffed at ideas of high-altitude trekking. Bah! He said. Trekking? I have climbed mountains, boys, mountains. He made like he'd been to half the six thousanders in India, wrestled with snow leopards, skied and para-jumped all over the place.

We were amazed. We were over-awed. Truly, O Master, we said, lead on, and show us the way, that we may walk in your steps and see the light. Amen.

All along that ride from Delhi through Chandigarh, Shimla district and into Kinnaur, he talked about how much he loved getting away to the hills, how much he felt at home, how much climbing made a different man out of him. We three looked at one another and felt dadgum lucky we had found a real authentic mountain champ to herd us along. Yes, I remember that ride.

So we were at Chitkul and it's a cute little place at about 3,400 metres, a bunch of hot Israeli women doping it up and maybe a shop or two. Perhaps by now it has become unvisitable. Sigh.

The first sign that things were not alright was when this chap pissed off the caretaker of the government rest house where we put up. As some of you doubtless know, hill people are particular about manners and etiquette. You can't talk to them like you would to a Delhi auto driver or someone. You got to watch your tongue. This guy didn't.

Then he began complaining about the food (which was good considering the nearest market was like a gadzillion miles away) and the bed (which was better than mine) and suchlike which was getting on our nerves.

First day climbing, and this chap refuses to get onto one of those dinky rope bridges where you sit in an iron basket and pull yourself across a gushing river. Great fun, but he would have none of it. Kind of derailed the general mood, you know.

Along comes evening, and we returned from another climb to find he was gone. Nope, said the caretaker (who made no secret of his dislike for the big guy), *I* haven't seen him. Don't ask *me*. We got worried, of course, seeing as it was a deserted sort of place and the Powers Above only knew what might happen to strangers in dark corners. About three hours later we found him in a small room upstairs in one of the houses with a bunch of random locals, watching a football game on the TV. He was a great fan of football, too.

And then, the following evening, we returned after some hard climbing to discover he had vanished with his car and almost all our luggage. Turns out he was sitting in the garden and he thought the mountains were falling on him or trying to eat him up or something. Craziest story I'd heard in a long time. Classic case of mountain-sickness.

Back in Delhi, we didn't see hide nor hair of him for weeks.

The good thing from all that was we were free to go our crazy ways and we went deep into Lahaul and Spiti district, visited a bunch of cave paintings and old Buddhist monasteries in the Tabo and Kaza town areas and had excellent adventures which I must have told you about endlessly and, as always, entertained you.

The other instance was back in college when I found myself on a beach in Daman with about a dozen guys and a girl. I knew some of the guys, the rest were friends of friends etc. and the first thing they did was to get roaring drunk and make a nuisance, which you mustn't in some parts of Daman because the locals are particular about it. So we were chased some distance down the blessed beach by a bunch of locals with sticks.

The girl was hot but you get my point. On the road, you better be with someone safe who won't lose his head and get you in trouble.

As usual, I go off substances a fortnight before the trip. I never drink on the road. You never know what you are getting into and it's best to have your head clear and focussed always, keep a low profile and both ears open. Besides, with so many things to see and experience, why'd anyone want to get drunk while journeying?

The other rule I have been trying to refine with each successive run is to travel light. I don't get where one has to carry half-a-dozen bags with potentially useless stuff. Get a precise idea of what you will need and try to minimise as much as possible, is what I say. Why'd you want to carry your house on your back?

What's that? Yes, you, nerdy-looking fellow with the goatee. You want figures? I kind of agree with the late revered Townie Whelen that a pack weight of six kilos is more than sufficient on any trip of a moderate duration. Townie Whelen laid down the six-kilo rule a hundred and twenty-odd years ago, and he used to carry *utensils* and ammunition with him. We have the advantage of lighter clothes and footwear and better travel conditions.

My pack weighs in at eight point two, including the comp and the camera, but I live in hopes of reducing it further.

In discussing the trip with my close friend S., I manoeuvre myself into a corner and end up promising him I won't do anything illegal this time. No bribes to border officials for various favours. Not even a peep across a border fence. I'm to leave the wire-cutter and shaded flashlight at home. No quiet word with the shady boys of the kind you-take-me-across-and-I'll-bring-back-something-useful. Looks like I'll have to walk the line, which puts a crimp into the plans—these places being the type where many options of breaking the law are available—but still.

Ed.: So. Shut the front door and get with the programme.

Don't worry: the rest of this story will be less about me and more about the particular narrowness of the narrow road.

TWO

I deeply detest waiting at airport luggage carousels. Perhaps you do, too. There are few more frustrating aspects of air travel than this. You get off the plane with maybe a backpack and off the bus and walk to the carousel, one smooth walk, all pepped up for the next stage. You position yourself at the curve where you can see both ends of the carousel, or at its beginning, where the luggage appears out of some mysterious twilight zone you will not be bothered to investigate. It does not make any difference where you position yourself because there isn't a scientific theory that can explain the Supreme Evil of the Black Rubber Carousel of Mordor.

Back before budget airlines turned airports into fishmarkets without the fish, it was marginally better, but just marginally. Today, because there are evil fiends lurking about who would snatch people's luggage mid-flight if they got a chance, the first thing you will see out of the twilight zone would be a couple of sad-looking suitcases that might or might not have been rejected by Gemelli Carreri himself. These here suitcases will have a sticker on top of them which will say 'I belong to XYZ Airways, are you sure you are picking up the right luggage?', which is part of some brilliant strategy the airlines cooked up to stop luggage thefts, haha. I'm serious, man. Haven't you seen them?

After these two decrepit pieces of airline property go their way, you pass the next millennia shifting your creaking trolley in one direction or another to adjust with your fellow travellers who will, naturally, believe your foot is part of the loose flooring. Along comes a gigantic Tourister in an insane electric blue colour. Voila! It belongs to no one at all, until it is about to disappear down the other end and some aunty says 'There it is, *beta,*' to a clueless kid half the bag's size who will then run after the dadgum bag and try to wrest it from the carousel unless physically restrained by more sober folk.

Following this arrives a procession of the weirdest bags and travelling accoutrements you have ever seen assembled in one place, which will make your eyes pop simultaneously. While you re-arrange your vision and frantically look around, the carousel goes suddenly empty. You panic. Are you at the right dadgum carousel, in the first place? Is your luggage now in Lakshadweep? Ahh, here comes the next batch, by which time you realise that handy carry-all with a fake brand tag you bought at knockdown rates at Sarojini Nagar market, was *also* bought, in the same colour, by half a million other idiots, of whom a random sample was on your flight. Never-ending entertainment on these occasions, if you ask me.

Which is why my pack is on my back and is cabin baggage.

There are two air routes from Delhi to Guwahati. One is direct. While you're boarding, take a quiet look around you. If there is a suspiciously large concentration of fat ladies on your flight, you'll be on the second route, passing through Bagdogra.

There is not much going for that route. On the contrary, the indirect flight path and stopover means an extra twenty minutes. The only good thing about it is, about an hour and twenty minutes in the air, if you look out the port windows and there is not much cloud, you can see Everest.

Bagdogra is on the chicken neck, the thin stretch of land that connects the North-east with the rest of the country and where you'll find a good-sized concentration of our armed forces, because just due south is Bangladesh, due north-east Bhutan and north-west, Nepal. Wait. I didn't need to spell all that out, did I? You can check the map and see for yourselves. The thing is, it is the nearest airport to Siliguri and connects to Gangtok, so you get the idea.

Most of the flight is made up of trader-type gents with appalling manners, accompanying the said fat ladies. I have never been able to determine, with reasonable accuracy, which of them are tourists and which are actual traders, so it is a sort of open question. I mean, *some* must definitely be tourists, seeing as there are so many usual tourist spots around. But why do they look like traders? Or is it that all the tourists who ever land at Bagdogra become, en route by touristy osmosis, trader-types. This must be a remarkable phenomenon if properly tested, you know. Reminds me of that demon character in that Neil Gaiman book, who discovers that all music cassettes and such kept in a car for like a fortnight or so eventually turn into *Queen* albums. Yeah, that book, man. This whole trader-type phenomenon is right next to it on the satanic scale, is what I say.

The matter of the gents' companions comes close behind on this scale. Sometime earlier, perhaps towards the beginning of aviation in India, some bright fellow must have grappled with this Curious Case of the Fat Ladies, and how best to solve it. Flights to Bagdogra, I've been told by highly-placed sources, are on specially designed secret super-alloy aircraft which withstand this weight concentration. The hostesses make sure the fat ladies are strapped in and no one gets up in case the aircraft loses its balance or whatever it is that helps in flying it. Is true, I swear.

There must have been a time when Bagdogra had what is called a native population. By 'a time' I refer, of course, to the early Bronze Age or thereabouts. Today the town is entirely t-t gents and fat ladies. At least the rest of us don't have to disembark.

Guwahati does not have facilities for landing at night, so in certain seasons, such as winters, what with the fog and early evenings, there is a relatively short window for all the flights. This is summer, just before the rains, when things are better.

Some time ago they made Guwahati an international airport, but there weren't many takers for it. The odd flight to Bangkok, maybe. Not anymore.

Over the green hills we swoop into the valley and the sight of the Brahmaputra gets people to crane their necks and follow its majestic path. It's a beautiful view. Take a good look. Back in the day, the Ahoms used to call the valley *Mong-Don-Sun-Kham*. In Assamese it becomes *Xunor Xophura* (and *please* don't ask me how to pronounce the 'x', work it out yourselves). The Golden Casket. They meant it, and not just because of the view.

While we are thus suspended, let me give you some facts about the region we are about to land in.

I'm assuming you'll get the capitals of all the seven states correct, so I'll pass over that. Seven, I said, because even though the government has clubbed Sikkim with the rest, it was not and never will be a part of what the North-east is all about. The region is an idea, a garland with some common history, some common languages, religions and ethnicity running all through it. You can't modify that on paper. However, if eight is what you want, eight it is, then. Sikkim is a fascinating place by itself.

Ed.: You've painted yourself into a corner here, you know, funny guy.

Erm. So. It covers an area of 255,168 sq. km, of which a large part in Arunachal is under or is claimed by the Chinese. Just consider the map for a moment (with an eye closed, for choice) and imagine it without the state boundaries. It is a vast place. In its extreme north-eastern corner is Arunachal, where the Himalayas end. To its south, over Nagaland and Manipur, is where the Patkai Range begins before it enters Myanmar. Except Assam, which comprises two big valleys and a hill district, and Tripura, the rest is hill terrain, which you probably know. I mean, you definitely know that, but it is not the whole of it, because the region is not all hills, as it is sometimes thought. Far from it. There are important valleys within these hills where a lot of humanity is concentrated. Manipur, for instance, lives almost entirely in the Imphal Valley deep within the hills. There are, of course, rivers all over the place.

Large swathes of the region are under thick forest, ranging from alpine vegetation in Arunachal and northern Nagaland to tropical and temperate elsewhere. There is a deal of rich biodiversity and possibly the last of the great forests of India house the last of several species. Particularly notable are rhinos, tigers, water buffalo, deer and elephants (the Big Five as conservationists call them), primates including the unfortunate hoolock gibbon, thousands of species of birds and insects and such varieties of trees, peoples, such varieties.

The region is supremely loaded with natural resources, specially oil, limestone, coal, natural gas and timber and, in Meghalaya, one of India's richest uranium deposits.

If you consider India, with its nearly 1,650 languages and dialects, a subcontinent, the North-east is a sub-subcontinent, with several hundred languages and dialects and a majestic array of ethnicity. About 150 of these dialects are spoken in Assam alone. Arunachal has fifty. Nagaland has fourteen major Naga tribes and they speak *sixty* different dialects. Get the idea?

Assam, Tripura and Manipur are mainly Hindu. Nagaland, Mizoram and Meghalaya are mainly Christian, and not just any Christian. For instance, percentage-wise, Nagaland has the highest concentration of Baptists in the world. Which place is second, you ask? The state of Missouri, in the US. Ha! Go boil an egg, rednecks!

Arunachal is mainly Buddhist.

Before we land, a quick word about something that bugs me no end. Don't try to deny it, because I know it is true. You meet someone from the North-east and if she or he looks Asiatic you use that horrible c-word and let it go at that. You have to understand: apart from Caucasoids and Australoids, there are different kinds of Mongoloids. They are as varied as you are. A Khasi from Meghalaya looks different from his neighbour, a Garo, also from Meghalaya. An Ao Naga from northern Nagaland is of a different stock to an Angami Naga, from southern Nagaland. If you look closely, a Malaysian is miles different from a Chinese or a Filipino, isn't he? Works the same way. To understand is to reach out, sayeth the master.

Six states are arrayed around Assam, so to get to any of them overland you got to go through Assam.

Today, Assam comprises the Brahmaputra Valley and, along the southern axis of its T-shape, the Barak Valley. Between these two is the hill district of Karbi Anglong. Historically, Assam has been of different shapes and sizes at different times, but its core was always the Brahmaputra Valley. During the golden age of the land, over the six hundred years that the Ahoms ruled their kingdom, it extended from the eastern border of the current Assam state to its western border, with the hill states in various kinds of tribute-paying arrangements.

Along came the Brits and made a few re-arrangements, including redrawing the maps (and boy, they were good at it, weren't they?) thus bringing in the present Meghalaya, Nagaland and Mizoram. After Independence, these hill districts went their separate ways, so we have Assam as we know it today.

Which, again, is in a state of flux and things of that sort. The Bodos, who have been around prolly since the last Neanderthals, want a separate state on the northern bank of the Brahmaputra, or (depending on which Bodo militant group has the microphone at the moment) a separate country. Karbi Anglong, already an autonomous hill district because the Karbis want to be on their own, has similar aspirations, and the last time I was in Assam I saw a map with some background talk about splitting the entire Barak

Valley away into another state, country or multinational corporation or some such. Don't ask.

Which brings us back to the core of Assam. It has, again historically, been in two distinct parts, the division this time based on the river itself. The land around the upper reaches of the Brahmaputra, from Dhemaji and Tinsukia districts in the east to Sonitpur and Nagaon districts midlength, was called Upper Assam, or *Ujoni Axom*. The valley west of this was Lower or *Namoni Axom*. It began as an administrative division, based on some differences in culture, practices and accents. Today the differences are more acute.

People from Upper and Lower Assam speak distinctly different versions of Assamese. Upper Assam has rich mineral reserves including coal, oil and natural gas plus vast expanses of tea estates. Lower Assam specialises in agricultural cultivation, strong Vaishnavite traditions and a people acknowledged as the more industrious and persevering of the entire valley. More on all these afterwards.

The place where we land is Guwahati airport. Guwahati itself is in Kamrup district, the easternmost part of Lower Assam (*are* you getting cross-eyed with all this geographical tap-dancing, dears? Please don't, or get a map from somewhere). Which is why you'll find most of the local residents of Guwahati, including those in the state's administrative departments, to be from Lower Assam.

Or something. The point I'm trying to make is we've landed, the weather looks just fine, I'll step out and smell the good old breeze of coming back home and take a look. There is much to see.

THREE

Guwahati is an ancient city. If you look at the history of cities, you'll usually find a very simple reason behind why they were set up at just that place, and not somewhere else. Like most old cities Guwahati is located near a river, to handle water and transport, which were *the* major urban headaches back then. Today's u.hs are transport and water, or the absence thereof, which seems to suggest a symmetry somewhere.

My theory is Guwahati came about because this is the narrowest point of the river. Along its run through the plains of Assam and into Bangladesh, the Brahmaputra turns from a fast mountain river into a broad and deep expanse. It retains its speed, though. Most of the stretch, particularly in western Assam and lower down, it's almost like a sea: so wide you can't see either bank if you are midstream.

At Guwahati it is about a kilometre and half broad, which sort of gives you an idea of how big it is. Here I should remind you (*sotto voce* in case the feminists in the audience get annoyed) that it is, after all, considered the only male river in the country, so there must be some reason the ancients thought of this connection.

Speaking of ancients, Guwahati back then was called Pragjyotishpura ('The City of Eastern Light'. God, must I translate everything for you?) and was a centre of much learning, particularly in astrology. It beats me how they did it, though: back when I was a kid and interested in astronomy, there was hardly much you could see in the skies, which were overcast whenever my friends and I walked up the hill near our place where the local physicists had put up this huuuge telescope.

It appears that the old place was also called Durjaya at some point in its admittedly badass history, and imho this is a nice name to have, seeing as it means 'invincible' (I think).

Ruled by different people, the capital of the Kamarupa kingdom seems to have been very famous. In the seventh century this side of Christ, Emperor Harsha Vardhana of Kanauj was pals with King Bhaskar Varman of Kamarupa and even sent across a bunch of Kanyakubja Brahmins to settle in central and western Assam. Many Assamese Brahmins derive their lineage from these people, they say.

Oh, which brings me to another side-note I was just waiting for. You see, there is a perpetual debate on about who or what the Assamese people are. Even agreeing that the Assamese are those who speak the Assamese language, there has been a fair bit of mixing down through time. There is the Mising tribe, for instance, which has been a big part of Assamese society for ages. They speak Assamese, there have been important cultural contributors from among them, they have all the same customs and even their folk dance is the same. There have been a few communities who have entered the state and assimilated completely. So what exactly does being an Assamese mean, and when did the people of Assam first emerge as a distinct entity?

History, clever chick that she is, at this point appears a little evasive. Archaeological evidence keeps emerging which not only proves that old continuously inhabited areas like

Guwahati were ancient urban areas, but also of being located along important trade routes, such as the southern Silk Route. Long as short, there are any number of theories.

The generally accepted one is the Caucasoid elements of Assamese society, including the upper castes, are, as mentioned above somewhere, descended from Brahmins from north India. Proof of this, it is said, are the *gotras* they carry. Now, I'm a little hazy about *gotras* and such, so I will not speak much on them, but how much you can rely on a common surname to prove descent is up for debate. So if Assam's history involves a bunch of north Indian Brahmins lugging their books and families through malarial swamps and hacking out a semblance of civilisation along the Brahmaputra, I'm all for it, because that is an interesting story to imagine, if not anything else.

But wait: as mentioned, the debate continues, and all kinds of arguments can be and are advanced. I heard this the other day which kind of rocked my cranium hard: the aforementioned theory is a big crock, some say. It was just advanced in the nineteenth century to show the rest of India (to which Assam had recently been added) that the Assamese upper castes were only cousins somewhat removed and, therefore, were equal. Hmm, could be a point there.

What rocked me even more was the corollary to this: that originally, the Assamese were not settlers from elsewhere but had been here all along and sort of only borrowed Vedic Hinduism. The wackiest sub-corollary is that Vedic Hinduism actually began in Assam and was exported to the rest of India and abroad, a kind of reverse flow of what we'd thought all along. I'm all for it, myself, plus a demand to shift the national capital to Guwahati. Although, on the kooky scale, this theory (which I hear is being seriously talked about by some academics) is right next to the one of that Brit writer fellow which claims that the world is ruled by a vast family of reptilian humanoids from another dimension. For, if we began Vedic civilisation in the Brahmaputra Valley, where did we come from in the first place, eh?

There are quite a few sites around the city with archaeological digs throwing up much evidence of settlement and culture from about the sixth century AD or earlier, and you've heard about the Kamakhya Temple, naturally. It has been an important centre of Mother Goddess worship for centuries. It is, in fact, the most sacred goddess temple in India. Yep, I read that in a Sanskrit text somewhere so I know it's true.

If you're the religious sort you might go up the hill on top of which the temple is. If you are *not* the religious sort you might still go up the hill, mainly because at its apex you get one of the most magnificent views of the Brahmaputra, which comes in on a wide arc from the east into a narrow funnel at the Guwahati banks, and then sort of widens out into the west. In summers you can see specks floating down the river, which might be groves of trees or houses swept away by the floods. In winter you will find siltbanks shining in the sun and tiny boats making the crossing. Which makes you wonder if, among the many reasons why the temple is where it is, one could have been that the ancients cannily camped at the most picturesque location they could find thereabouts.

The road uphill used to be an entertaining ride till just

a while back, with a bunch of hairpin bends and nothing to catch the vehicle in case of a mistake, but it is wider and less fun today.

Now, there are many legends behind why Kamakhya is such an important Mother Goddess zone, but mainly it is an underwater spring that froths up at the meeting point of two peaks, and you can have as many Freudian sessions as you want with that because the ancient books, with which you, being wise, are acquainted, have a lot to say about Shiva dancing with his wife's body and all that.

Around this here spring is built the temple, although it is not a very ancient structure, since it was built and destroyed a few times. The last time it was built, on the designs of the previous structure, was in the late sixteenth century. The architecture is similar to some other temple constructions, with a rising pinnacle over the inner sanctum connected to a stretched, squat wing. This wing has a roof the locals call 'tortoise-backed', with the four eaves sloping in a regular curve fourways. This design is found in other temples of that period and the logic behind it is instantly observable: the curves drain out rainwater quickly, making the stone structure remarkably durable.

Since I have about run out of whatever little architectural knowledge I have, I will now tell you a story to illustrate a point which I feel is significant but which may turn out to be just fluff.

And the point I shall now illustrate is that, imho, Hinduism does not really have a concept of evil. At least not on the lines of evil in monotheistic religions. Satan and his Judeo-Islamic counterparts are suitable examples of hate-figures for some righteous smiting now and then that

God and his people carry out. Sometimes, the evil that humans conjure on their own is far more hardcore than even these people, but in a theological debate, you can prop up old Iblis (ha, I *knew* I'd remember the Islamic name!) and have a reasonably sound basis for an old-fashioned good-and-evil deathmatch anytime.

Hinduism, sadly, has *asuras*. Now, some of these guys were doubtless wicked folk, given to the odd war against the gods and raids on Brahmins (which I sometimes vaguely consider taking personally), but they also spent a deal of time praying to the Trinity and thinking up wholly ingenious ways to be immortal, indestructible Mega-Terminators only to be pwned, Wile E. Coyote-style, by some appalling loophole in their wishes which they, being smart, should have seen coming.

I mean, Ravana is supposed to be the bad guy, right? And yet here we have a semi-demon who could play a musical instrument with his *intestines*, create a Wagnerian original hymn to Shiva and recite the Vedas from end to end and other such mind-bending things. Our sixth day of the week is named after the Gandalf of the asuras, remember?

The other point which I'm trying to arrive at is Hindu gods could be so juvenile sometimes, with their machinations and things. They could show a bit more dignity here and there, is what I think. Would make it easier to look up to them, you see.

Narakasura was one such demon king back in the day, ruler of Kamarupa and an overall supreme hard-as-nails sort of dude who looked at the world, wanted it all and made sure he got it, too.

Respected and feared by his people and the gods, Narakasura, by various accounts which I have not read but heard third- or fourth-hand, was also very direct in his approach, for those times. So this one time, he fell in love with Goddess Kamakhya herself.

Now, an ordinary chap, on falling in love with a goddess (even though the goddess is located within his kingdom) would go off and text goofy messages to himself and get drunk till he'd cleared the thing out of his system, or go about lurking and muttering and avoiding human contact in case someone told him, sternly, to not be an ass and move on.

Narakasura, however, was made of industrial-quality tempered steel. So up the hill he went, knocked on the goddess's door, and when she came out, proceeded to lay his heart at her feet and profess a lot of (presumably) mushy stuff which did not go into the records and which therefore I do not have to repeat here, which would have been icky for me because I am a conscientious narrator and don't like cutting corners, however mushy the corners may be.

The goddess, on hearing what must have essentially been on the lines of 'I am the dude on this here block, as far as eye can see, with countless subjects, gold and precious jewels and power beyond even the gods, so what say?' thought a bit and said that it was a good offer, and she was very impressed. But, she said, Naraka would have to prove his love for her, or she would disappear.

Not realising that he had walked right into the middle of a *Looney Tunes* episode, Naraka said he would do anything she commanded him to do, anything at all in the world. So the goddess told him: my devotees have to climb this sheer hill to worship me. Make it easy for them. Build a stairway from the base of this peak to the top. By yourself. In. One. Night.

And Naraka, mighty, invincible, hardcore . . . did it.

Now, in the happy days of my childhood, I have been up and down that stairway multiple times. It is easy to see that it is much older than the 400-year-old temple, and is today mossy and overgrown with creepers, but the stairs are giant slabs of stone and will be around for a long time yet. You can just imagine the nature of a man (sorry, demon) who carted these slabs on his back or otherwise and placed them up the hill.

And the goddess watched Naraka build her stairway and realised that this man (sorry, demon) had meant every word of what he'd said. The books don't tell us what she thought in those moments, with the rest of the night stretching away and the stairway almost finished. The books never tell us what the gods really thought.

Did she wonder why no god ever showed that kind of courage? Did she wish that things had been other than the divine mandate that demons *have* to be the bad guys and therefore beyond the pale? We do not know.

What we do know is what she did.

She did what most gods seem to have done when the stuff was about to hit the fan. She dialled Vishnu. And Vishnu, ever the nice fellow to help his colleagues sort out situations just like this, turned himself into a rooster, or, in other versions, commanded a rooster to crow, so that dawn would arrive before the demon finished his job.

Naraka, just a few dozen feet from the top, heard the

rooster crow and killed the fowl. Later, he was killed by Krishna's wife for stealing someone's earrings which is a highly dumb way for a story (and such a person) to end and must have been heavily edited by the gods in a very subtle manner which I have not yet been able to piece together.

Everything went back to as it was except the pilgrims, who might have benefitted from the staircase, had to hack it the last few feet to the top and might or might not have wished that Naraka had been allowed to at least complete it before the gods intervened.

Guwahati, of course, was big back then and the capital of the Kamarupa kingdom, somewhere making a very smooth transition from legend into confirmed history, like the other ancient cities of India. When Hiuen Tsang dropped in to have a few words with King Bhaskar Varman, Pragjyotishpura was about 20 km long and a big naval base with thousands of ships. Tsang being a sober traveller and objective observer, I'll believe what he had to say (plus a vision of his 'Pragjyotishpura's 20,000 ships of war' patrolling the river down to the Bay of Bengal and beyond is a lovely one). Although there is the possibility that Tsang, being scholar-like and not, say, with the kind of military-diplomatic background of Megasthenes, might have called some dinky boats naval ships and sort of assumed it did not make much of a difference. But it is undeniable that Kamarupa was a big military power.

Another reason why Guwahati was consistently a strategic location down the line has to do with the Silk Route. You see, as you perhaps know, there were two distinct and separate routes which jointly formed what we know today as the Silk Route. The first of these began from eastern China, went directly due west over northern Tibet, Central Asia, the Middle-east and Turkey before splitting in two. One route went over the Bosporus into Europe, the other took to the Mediterranean Sea before reaching Spain. This line was hit the most during the Crusades, Mongol raids, Ottoman Turkish expansion and all the minor skirmishes and differences of opinion which kind of presaged the Middle-East mess as we know it today.

But there was a second route, with an equally interesting history, because it was not only a trade route and affected by the rise and fall of nations, but also led to a lot of migration and formation of cultures in the parts of the world it passed through.

This route, like the first, emerged from eastern China, fed by ever-growing swathes of mulberry plants, busy worms and porcelain kilns, but went south over the basins of the great Chinese rivers before hitting Vietnam. Here it turned west into Laos, a country which you barely get to hear of today but is worth taking a look at because back then there was barely anyone in this part of the world who had not heard of the people there.

From Laos great caravans filled with goods used to pass through the forests and the even-then-intensively cultivated rice plains of central Thailand and Myanmar before crossing the Patkai Range into the North-east. Passing through the Brahmaputra Valley, these caravans went through northern India into Afghanistan and central Asia or, alternately, took to the sea in India and moved directly to Egypt or Arabia.

The Silk Route touched the parts of the world it went

through in subtle economic ways, which tend to leave as much a mark as conquests and stuff. In the Brahmaputra Valley, it led to the cultivation of the *muga* silkworm, from which the beautiful cloth you might have seen somewhere is derived. A short distance from Guwahati is Sualkuchi where the best craftsmen in these kinds of silk still live today and carry on the legacy of a time when crafts from countries you would never hope to see in, like, three lifetimes, were being transmitted around Eurasia. There are other centres in Lower Assam known locally and perhaps in the country for metalwork, such as copper alloys, another prized craft from that time. Now you know.

However, the best-kept secret of the southern Silk Route is the Road of Jars. Now, strain yourself, peoples, to remember whether you've heard of it somewhere, you know, *some* reference to it. Have you? Ahh, thought so. Listen up.

In north-central Laos is a big plain. There is nothing geologically remarkable about it, but it is dotted with several thousand stone jars. Big stone jars, man-sized. Some of them are empty, some have crystals and ornament pieces still within them. Today it might be a bit difficult for you to check these stone jars in detail, because there was a big-time civil war in Laos back in the early Sixties, and the Plain of Jars, as locals called it, eventually became one of the most heavily-mined areas in south Asia. This itself is a major, though dubious, distinction, since Laos's neighbour, Cambodia, has more landmines than can be defused in the next century.

Now, the Plain of Jars leads off towards the west, so if you follow it (without, of course, stepping on the mines) you will come across stone jars, identical in make and size, in Myanmar as well. The Road of Jars ends in south Assam's Cachar Hill district where, in the odd wilderness ravine or gulch, you might even today come across a mouldy old man-sized jar full of moss and rainwater and maybe a few medieval trinkets.

Not many people have studied the Road of Jars, but there was this one woman anthropologist in the Fifties who did. Come on, if I remembered her name, wouldn't I tell you? Anyway, the theory is these jars were used to store clean water for the caravans along the southern Silk Route. Alternately, they could have been receptacles for offerings of precious trinkets for a safe journey, good business and such. I do not know if similar jars were found along the northern Silk Route.

But we return.

With the rise of the Ahoms in the thirteenth century, the capital of Assam shifted to the east and Guwahati became a much-contested frontier town. It was captured and freed from the Mughals multiple times till the Brits came on the scene, spelt the town as Gauhati, made Shillong the capital of Assam and this town its plains sister city.

Travellers to the region will remark immediately on the absence of ancient monuments here. This is due to a combination of reasons. Some parts, such as Nagaland and Mizoram, have never been under kings (and only nominally under neighbouring kingdoms who were more interested in tribute reaching their capitals than in going uphill and building palaces). Hill tribes, republican and taken up with the perils of combining a hunter-gatherer lifestyle with the vagaries of the climate, did not go in for the 'halls of stone' kind of statement. So tribal meetings were held out in the open and if anyone wanted to impress visitors, a few heads or trophies of war were considered as compelling a message as an arch or a mausoleum or something.

Valley and plains kingdoms like in Assam, Manipur and, specifically, Tripura, did some building, but only when the mood took them, and most of this was functional. Besides, there was not much they saw in taking years to build what could be in ruins with the next big earthquake, which is common there. And there have been some big ones in the past. And by big I mean 8.2 and such. So architecture sort of had to adjust to that.

Guwahati, if you take a look around, therefore does not have many old structures, and hardly any pre-dating the Brits. If, say, you took a drive down the road which parallels the Brahmaputra and approached the old city at a place called Panbazar, you'd see a big structure along the bank. It is a gate with twelve arches, and most average Guwahatians, as I know for certain, might not be able to tell you its name, so they should read this story as well, just in case someone asks them, for this gate marks a defining moment in the setting of a kingdom and the rise of an empire.

Assam came under the Brits in 1826 after the Treaty of Yandaboo, but it was not a simple matter of the redcoats waltzing in and saying 'Eh, what' and dropping their aitches. It was a gradual process of coming to grips with a vast, complicated land. By the time the second wave of Brits moved in in 1841, they were horrified to discover that not only did the natives live in mud-and-thatch houses, but the early Brits, realising the merit of light-weight construction during earthquakes, had been living likewise.

In the next thirty years, the only pukka houses built in Guwahati would be two annexes to the local court. Things were thus in 1874, when the Governor-General of India himself, a certain Lord Northbrook, decided to take a look at Her Majesty's easternmost Indian province and, while he was at it, to see where all that dadgum tea was coming from, eh?

This news, as we can imagine, did not sit too well with our Brit friends and their native assistants in Guwahati. They looked at each other and did the 'parting lips and straining eyes' number, because Northbrook would have to be put up in style, or they'd be shipped to someplace far worse.

They did some improvising and decided, very cleverly I should say, to convert the Commissioner's office itself into a residence, thus saving on new construction and building up from the only presentable structure in town.

But that was hardly enough now, was it? Northbrook needed to be given a state welcome first. So they scratched their heads some more till one wise Brit whacked the designs of the chapel at King's College back on their home island and built it, arch for arch, on the riverbank. Thus the Northbrook Gate came up, hosted the Governor-General, and all was well for his harried underlings afterwards, as far as the records reveal. The private comments of Northbrook himself on his accommodations are not available on record—which is probably for the best.

The Northbrook Gate, built in 1874 of brick, thus has

the distinction of being the oldest structure still standing in Guwahati.

It was not, however, the oldest stone-and-brick structure, nor was it the grandest back then. If you proceeded further into the old part of Guwahati down Panbazar and got directed to the century-plus Cotton College, you'd find, in a cute little garden opposite the college, a cute little church with sloping tin roofs. This is the Christ Church, today made of half-brick and elephant grass and a hundred and seven years old. But that is only the second half of the story.

Back in the 1830s, the Brits were going east big-time and getting the hang of the tea business, so there were a lot of planters, adventurers and mercenaries putting up at Guwahati. Some of these were even (surprise, surprise) religious, so they got together, took out donations and got a church built. Completed in 1850, the first version of the Christ Church had a huge square tower in the best Brit midland tradition and the trappings of the Church of England inside it. It had a wide front porch where aforesaid planters, adventurers and mercs and their ladies could swap a few tales and swat bugs.

The church had not been up four years when along came the next big earthquake and levelled it right to the ground.

I got to tell you about these three quakes, okay, because they were big ones. The only reason not many people died in the valley, comparatively, that is, was the mud-and-elephant grass huts they used to live in, which kind of goes to show, once again, that in a new kind of land, borrowing a few tips from the locals can save lives. I mean, brick structures had no chance at all with these mega-quakes.

The 1854 one was never measured, you know, seeing as they didn't have instruments for this back then, but geologists and other smart people who study earthquakes have this other system I heard of somewhere, something to do with measuring displacement and cracks in the earth and such, from which they can come up with fairly accurate estimates.

This sounds like an excellent idea, although you might not find me measuring a sudden freakin' crack in the earth for the interests of science or whatever. That's the last thing you'd think of after an earthquake, isn't it? I mean, it's not like: 'Oh, ho, ho, there's a crack in the earth so I will stand over it with a tape and get its measure down to the nth inch' or 'Ahh, that was a good earthquake. I will now stand under this here building or very unstable hill and measure the displacement herefrom.' But it seems there *are* people who do that, so there is no accounting for taste.

So, anyway, that quake pushed past 8 on the Richter scale, and with it went the Christ Church, which is sad, because it was beautiful.

Well, no one said pioneering was easy, so another round of donations were made and it was built up again, stone by stone, with a few small alterations to the design.

You'd think that was that, but wait, dude. In 1897 came *another* earthquake, this time an even bigger one. Some say that, on the Richter scale, it measured nearly 8.3, making it among the top-of-the-quakes list in recorded history. Not as many people died as might be expected, mainly because of said lightweight construction, but Christ Church fell to pieces once again, and remained so until the Brits got the point and built what is called an 'Assam-type' house with sloping tin roofs, and that one stands today.

This new structure is, barring a few changes here and there, what you'll get to see, and it has passed the quake test with credit to its designers, and how. Because the third, and the worst, was yet to come.

This was in 1950: half a century later, more people, more modern houses and buildings and such. The quake, too, was an upgraded version. Y'see, it was a bit more than 8.6, the seventh-strongest (highest? worst? dunno what's the proper adjective: it's by magnitude so you decide) temblor in the whole of human history, with or without the dadgum R-scale. It was also much better documented than the previous two.

It began from this place called Medog, right on the Arunachal-Tibet border, on Independence Day. That place must have simply turned turtle or something. Later there'd be pilots who saw the whole thing from the air, and it must have been a sight. They saw entire plains shifting, they saw hills sliding down, they said later various geographical landmarks they knew from earlier had become unrecognisable. I've seen some pics these fliers took. Scary.

Anyone here know what a seiche is? Anyone? Okay, it is this dinky wave inside a closed body of water, like a pond or a bathtub, a kind of wave in a normally waveless body, you know. Mostly it comes from earthquakes.

So, get this: there were seiches in freakin' Norway because of Medog. The last time that happened must have been that super-volcano in Indonesia, you know the one which blew off that island in the nineteenth century, whashisname. Yeah. That one.

So imagine what it must have been on the ground. They say fish were thrown out of the water, and that's a fact. The earth opened up, the works. A little more than 1,200 people died, which you'd say was few for such an event, although it was still massive for such a thinly-populated area.

But the absolutely worst result of Medog was the floods. You see, as you'll find when we reach the east Assam town of Dibrugarh, the rivers changed their courses, and their beds were pushed up. The banks fell into the torrents, the tributaries got choked with mud and got dammed. Consider Subansiri, a major tributary which flows down south from Arunachal. Like an entire range of hills fell into it in a few minutes, and it was so much that the river got blocked.

If you ever visit the Subansiri (which you should because the people in the villages around it are great hosts and there are some excellent angling areas) you'll find this very fast mountain river in a great hurry, so you can imagine the amount of earth which must have fallen into it.

But while the other rivers cleared their dams in a few hours or so, the Subansiri was dammed for more than a week or something. When waters finally broke through, they went out in waves more than 22 feet high, like megagallons of water. Subansiri took more than 500 people with it, and the place was never the same.

Neither was the Brahmaputra, because this is when the floods became worse than ever, and they've never stopped.

The story of Medog is also the story of this guy Kingdon-Ward. The poor fellow was a botanist doing his business up in a place called Rima in Arunachal, just a bit from Medog. Well, I doubt he got much botanicking done because the hills started falling all around him, and he made it back to civilisation by the enamel of his teeth or something.

Not a minute before he got back and realised he had been sitting on one of the worst earthquakes in history and *the* most geographical alterations from a single quake ever. But did Kingdon-Ward have a chance? Ha, you think so? He wasn't back in Assam before the scientists, finding out he was their only rep at the epicentre, were over him like flies, asking damn-fool questions like 'What was the exact effect at the epicentre' and 'What did you see' and 'What did it feel like' and such, like those idiot TV reporters do these days, which sucks.

So what could poor Kingdon-Ward do? He turned around and told them, very gently from what I hear, that he was a botanist, and had been looking at the trees and stuff, and during Medog he had been reluctantly compelled to halt this activity because he was being rolled around on the ground trying to avoid a peak landing on his head, so, unfortunately, he had not had the opportunity to make seismic-geological observations, although he would have totally *loved* to, indeed, and was even then thinking of returning to the spot for another round. And if that did not shut them up, I do not know if anything ever did.

But that wasn't the only quake just then, because aftershocks continued for like weeks, and they were 6 and up, so overall it was a very crappy time.

And from these three mega-quakes we have something we grew up with in Assam, which is called the 50-Year Theory. Now, if you have observed closely, what with 1854, 1897 and 1950, these mega-quakes were hitting at intervals of a half-century each time. It stood to reason that the next big one would hit at the turn of the century, give or take a few years.

Figuratively speaking, Assam was quaking under the quilt from about 1995 for like a decade.

Ed.: I can think of one person, at least.

It wasn't a good time, I can tell you that.

The big one never came, though, which possibly explains why, just a few years later, the valley and particularly Guwahati has been into constructing these huge buildings all over the place. Sort of making up for lost time and geological paranoia, as some people dismiss it. I just hope the theory is wrong.

Meanwhile, back in Guwahati and talking about the Christ Church, there are a few other structures totally worth taking a look at, including the old Ugratara Temple down Lamb Road, which we will visit in a bit. I'm feeling a bit introspective at the moment, so bear with me. Deep thoughts coming right up, man.

FOUR

You never really understand how deep the words 'home' and 'homeland' are till you've been away for some time. I've been away for more than a decade, barring short vacations and when I worked with a newspaper here. I won't describe the feeling, mainly because I might not do it properly and besides you understand what I'm talking about.

The best part of returning to Guwahati are the Boys. I went to this boys' school there, you see, and an unwritten tradition is if you're batchmates there, you are friends for life. Not a tradition, actually. That would imply an element of imposition or formality. It just happens, you know. It's unconditional and deeply, deeply elemental. You walk down a street in some arbit city and up pops this guy who looks familiar except he's taller or has put on weight or lost some hair or is with this awesome woman or something, and you go 'Aren't you . . .?' and he goes 'It's you, you . . .' (the rest being in most cases unprintable) and you pick up the conv. thread right from where you left it. You don't need to put on an act, you don't need to remind yourself who you are, you don't need to put the guard up because this guy knew you since before you started wearing long trousers and he can see right inside to who you really are. That kind of thing. And no-one ever really stops being in touch.

The Boys still in the city drop in and (this being home base) a lot of spiritual discussions take place by the end of which everyone is sloshed witless and I watch everything and ask myself, as I do each time I return: what am I doing elsewhere, I should be here. Since I am, I might as well make the most of it.

They shake their wise old heads on hearing about my travel plans but don't stop me. It'll be good fun, they say, when you return to tell us what happened. I meet some new friends of theirs, there is a bit of jamming with a guitar and a tabletop (I think there was just the one guitar but I am not sure, I might have been seeing double because I was on my way to this epic bender to compensate for the time to come on the road) and this new guy with a good singing voice comes up with a parody of Assamese nursery rhymes that's so hilarious, seriously, if you knew the original songs you'd die laughing. There is a bit of talk about bringing out an album with these songs and N., a Boy who lives in Delhi but is on vacation here records it on his cellphone for our subsequent entertainment. Which reminds me: N., I hope you didn't delete the recording. Wait, you do remember we recorded it, don't you?

This other night, at about 1, I was sitting in a car with my friend G., near the Gauhati Medical College watching a line of trucks carrying river sand to a place they were filling up. G. and I were talking about how much that stretch had changed. 'It was all swamp earlier,' G. remarked, to which I reminded him that most of that part of the city, as we knew it growing up, was swamp.

In fact, the whole of Guwahati was swampland crossed by hills, except a few high-lying areas near the river.

Today, Guwahati is India's third-fastest growing city and among the top eighty in the world, which means the swamps, which used to be catchment areas for rainwater overflow, are being filled up and high-rises of reflector glass and suchlike are coming up faster than an occasional prodigal can keep up with. There used to be this big swamp in west Guwahati called Deepor Beel (a *beel* being what we call a swamp). It was 4,200 square hectares big. Today it is 10 per cent of this. Ten per cent, man, and prolly shrinking faster. The disappearance of these drainage areas is one reason Guwahati is perpetually water-logged in the monsoons, but at the rate at which the trees around are being processed into timber and the hills into earthfill, we've taken care of the monsoons as well, so no one needs to worry at all.

There's this new apartment complex, okay, and when I heard the price tag for each apartment I said: 'But that's expensive even for Delhi!' Each time I return I'm like 'When did that come up?' or 'What happened to this road?'

One of the cons of returning home after a while is the place has changed while you weren't there. It is inconsiderate of the place, if you ask me. The reason you love your home is it is a set of certain things, including houses, streets, traffic, people. You know: personality. And you return and you hardly recognise the place anymore and you feel kind of let down, by your memory, if not anything else. One expects the place to remain a museum in perpetual stasis, a logical but nevertheless selfish expectation. Guwahati, bursting at the seams with new shopping centres, multiplexes and vehicles, is filled with the hum of construction and industry, and hurries on.

Some people I meet point out one aspect of all this

which worries people familiar with Assam's economy. It's not like the state has hit a revenue stream jackpot or found itself, Saudi-style, floating on a mini-ocean of high-grade dinosaur remains. The economy remains as it always has: shaky. Agricultural production isn't exactly booming. There is no sudden spurt of manufacturing industries. Only services have seen some growth: mainly in banking and insurance (which, between us, is expected, seeing as Guwahati is the centre of the North-east and these two sectors are growing in the region).

All of which leads to this: where has this new-found prosperity and growth come from, eh? Some, definitely, from all the money siphoned and stashed away by bureaucrats, cops and contractors over decades of well-meaning but unsupervised Central largesse. Some boldness with the waning of insurgency and most of the top ULFA leaders in the slammer (I was *waiting* to use that word). But is this growth sustainable? Will the numerous new and shiny showrooms of high-end products and precious metals continue to show profits? Will easy EMIs of Rs 2,500 per compact car continue to unleash new owners on the streets per diem? That is a question that the 800,000-and-rising Guwahatians will have to answer sooner than they think.

My favouritest part of Guwahati as it is today is old Guwahati, which is not to say it looks like . . . Old Delhi, or Old Hyderabad. The stretch from Panbazar to Uzanbazar skirting the southern bank of the river has been around in its present form for more than a hundred years. At least the layout and other things have not changed. You'll find administrative offices and other installations here, on the same site, and sometimes in the same building, that the

Brits made. The roads are narrow for today's traffic, but if you find yourself walking near Dighalipukhuri, the big lake behind the Gauhati High Court, and find yourself in Lamb Road, look around you. You'll find a lot of cute little single-storey houses with windows all over the place with quart-pane glass and tin roofs. Today a lot of these houses are being demolished for apartment blocks, but yes, this stretch still has vestiges of what the city used to be. Rather like a quiet, dignified, well-preserved old lady, sitting at a riverbank.

The rest of the place has, as I said, changed a lot. It has changed so rapidly and conclusively that even people who return more frequently than I do feel a certain displacement walking the streets. More traffic, new houses, people even talk differently.

I kind of get annoyed with this whole homogenisation business that urban spaces in India are getting into. Now every town and city looks like every other. I suppose it is inevitable, but I wish cities could retain some of their distinctive individuality amid all this.

The good news is, Guwahati now looks like your city (and yours too, ma'am, over there, thanks for asking), so you won't feel like a stranger.

Among the more usual collateral damage to all this progress business are latchkey kids. Back when we were small, sure, both our parents worked and all, but they had time for us. Time and consideration. I don't entirely understand what happened, because it's not like the city has expanded majorly and takes up commuting time, but young working parents have progressively lesser time for their children.

I go meet the most respected journalist in the North-east, my former editor at *The Sentinel* newspaper, and he tells me about this case which came to his daughter, a noted child specialist. This little boy dipped half-a-dozen of the crispest mosquito repellant tablets in tea and ate them all and had to be rushed to hospital puking all over himself. It seems his parents got around to noticing him after he had been there and done that. The doctor told the parents, very rightly, I think, that they were lucky they were in India: in any other country they'd be in prison for negligence. I hope parents settle down and spend time with their children, because nothing else is as important.

Returning to G. and me in a car near the Gauhati Medical College. That part is on the G.S. Road. A few years back, when I was with *The Sentinel*, the six-or seven-storey Income Tax office dominated the skyline on G.S. Road. A few commercial complexes and old-style houses dotted the stretch. Today it is completely unrecognisable and bright at night, filled with crowds dining out or shopping or otherwise taking part in whatever.

While on the matter of infrastructure, I have to tell you that the roads, which today can only be seen clearly late at night, have been substantially improved because of the National Games a few years ago, before which there were, shall we say, a lot of problems. Today at least the main roads are in very good shape, although the drains are up to their usual business, which brings me to Guwahati's city sport.

Every city, I believe, has a unique sport that goes with it, something cooked up by that city's unreplicable combination of culture, attitude and street rules. Unreplicable is the key word here: the sport sort of defines the city. For instance, New York has emphatically chosen mugging. San Francisco provides you the sport of being accosted by random hot women in tie-dye dresses or some such with donation boxes for some ecological foundation or the other. In Melbourne you can now participate in muggings, provided you are an Indian *and have an iPod.*

Guwahati's city sport is Falling into Storm Drains. You see, back in the dark ages, that is, in the late Seventies or thereabouts, the city fathers decided to solve the annual waterlogging problem by building, along the three arterial roads of G.S. Road, Zoo Road and M.R.D. Road, two parallel lines of storm drains, which are sort of wide and deep drains designed, on paper, to flush out tonnes of silt and rainwater in the snap of a finger into the Bharalu river which runs through the city and thus into the Brahmaputra.

This was the plan and it, predictably, has never worked. The logged water (or whatever it is you call all that water during a waterlogging) does not spontaneously enter the drains because the entry points, by the time the rains come in, are choked with garbage. The streets overflow, the drains ditto, and there is not a wise soul that can tell which is which. So every monsoon you have random people disappearing around you into an open storm drain and you have to negotiate the flooded roads or the footpaths built over the drains with great care. Though citizens have since my childhood threatened everything from a municipal tax boycott to violent vigilante action against these man-eating storm drains, matters continue as they were.

Once in a while however, amid this tragedy, there does shine out a ray of hope that perhaps there is a good and just creator with an appreciable sense of irony still on duty up there. Man, I got to tell this story.

I did my 12th from Cotton College, and one of the people who taught us was this insufferable little fellow who was determined to be a pain to all manner of life-forms that he came across, students being the lowest in his book. Not only was he hilariously inane in class, he could also be seen in public life in various activist capacities, as well as in the papers where he wrote vitriolic little letters to the editor on all the ills he could see in the world. One of the high points of my journalistic career was back in 2004 during the Parliamentary elections when he, standing up in what must have been a thoroughly misjudged moment of delusion, brought in 5,000-odd votes and lost his deposit.

So, anyway, a few years ago he was taking a walk down Chandmari during the rains, when a lurking open manhole did what countless Cottonians had fantasised about for generations. I know you're going to yell at me for saying this, but I absolutely must: 'Accoutred as he was, he plunged in.'

He was then fished out of six feet of sludge and Frooti tetrapacks by pedestrians, diagnosed with a sprained ankle and sent to the Gauhati Medical College. So far he had managed with marginal damage, but at GMC his luck ran out, because a press photographer had dropped in for a chat with some doctor friend of his, heard the rumour, popped into his ward and snapped a picture which my friends and I will treasure forever. In the inside pages of *The Assam Tribune*, across three glorious columns, was our man, with a plastered leg and a priceless expression on his face. The caption made my week.

G.S. Road stands for Guwahati-Shillong Road. It starts from the city and snakes up into the hills of Meghalaya to ... where else, eh? Come along.

FIVE

Geography Lesson 101: Know what a pop-up is?

A pop-up is a mountain or hill formation that rises from a level plain. It is not connected to any other range or formation. It is, simply, there.

Imagine a car crash. The twisted metal, the irregular shapes created by the impact. The Himalayas are the result of a super-omega collision, as we know, its peaks swept up by the impact of the Deccan plate with the rest of Asia. The Himalayas, in the northwest, connect with the Hindu Kush. In the east and north, with the Tibetan plateau, in the south, with the Patkai. The Himalayas are not pop-ups. They are dents on a geological megavehicle after the pile-up of the mega-annum (which is what a million years is called, so you needn't look it up on your cellphones, I can see a few people surfing from here, man).

Guwahati is built around several pop-up hills, though. These are reserve forests today (but there is a lot of encroachment etc. going on). These are big hills.

But the great-grandfather of pop-ups is due just south of Guwahati. The hill range we know as Meghalaya is the biggest pop-up in this part of the world. South and west is Bangladesh, with its plains and river distributaries. East, again, is Assam. Meghalaya rises out of the plains and ends in the plains. As I said, it simply is.

Till some time ago, going back to a crowded area in Guwahati called Paltanbazar, you could get on a bus and go to Shillong over the G.S. Road.

The wise (b-i-i-g question mark here) old men of Assam's capital decided, however, to decongest the city, so they built this humungous Inter-State Bus Terminus. They then looked at each other, smiled wickedly, and put that aforementioned ISBT in the back of beyond, next to a national highway miles from Guwahati. So, you catch another bus to reach this place before you leave for Meghalaya, or anywhere else.

G.S. Road, where it hits the hills of Meghalaya, used to be great fun back in the day: parts of it kept falling off or caving in, so rutted and pitted and narrow that you kind of asked yourself why anyone tarmacked it and didn't leave it as it used to be a hundred-odd years ago, a horse and bullock cart track over which the Brits used to strain their backs getting to Shillong, their beloved Scotland of the East. The Brits were great at euphemisms and quick at finding summer getaways, weren't they?

Meghalaya can be broadly divided into three parts—from west to east, Garo Hills, Khasi Hills and Jaintia Hills. Each part named after the tribe which lives there. Shillong is in the Khasi Hills.

Shillong is built around three hills which, in the days before the Brits, were sacred for the Khasis. (Like most other tribes in the region, Khasis, before Christ came calling, were animists.) By sacred I mean sacred, alright? Like a living entity or something. Which meant they were very careful about preserving it and such. They made sure the place retained its habitat and eco-system or whatever it is places are supposed to have, you know, trees, streams, animals, the works.

Today Shillong is all concrete and jazzy cars which zip up and down cute little hill roads at deplorable velocities. Indeed, one misses the wood-panelled floors of one's childhood; the houses on wooden pillars, the ground floor an open area for pigs, cars and suchlike; the really cold winters when water pipes used to freeze in an instant and you took a rod or something and hit the pipes to the desired effect. Winter in Shillong today is a letdown.

There is much to see in Shillong, which still retains vestiges of its Brit past, back when it used to be the capital of the whole of Assam. Shillong continued to be Assam's capital till 1972, when Meghalaya was formed and Assam's capital shifted to Guwahati.

So you can take a walk down Police Bazaar, have great momos (real momos, not the fake ones you've had all your lives), various kinds of insects at the weekly market, feed those beautiful carp at Ward's Lake, go down to the Beedon-Bishop Waterfalls and just sit and listen to the water cascade down. Or you can go to church and hear some awesome choir music, 'myes. The church plays a big role in society, even in politics, in Meghalaya, Nagaland and Mizoram, but its best part are the choirs. You just go to church and listen, and will feel the breeze in the evenings swirl quietly around you and you don't need to read *The Book of Balance and Harmony* or something which might or might not show you how to sort out your life and you'll say, let me just sit here some more, I can always go to whichever place I am headed for later. Let me just listen.

Music runs through the hills and valleys of the Northeast in such deep and rich veins, it constantly throws up surprises. There is folk, for one: each ethnic group and people has its own music, its own special instruments. There is rock, for another.

I haven't looked too deeply into the whys, but I guess church choirs have a big role behind how rock music first took hold in these parts. There are bands, and good bands, at that, on virtually every street. You walk down a lane and a bunch of guys on a verandah are jamming, their very souls poured into their instruments, the music perhaps familiar, maybe that band you listen to occasionally, eh? Then you step onto the aforementioned verandah and strike up a conversation and maybe pick up the guitar and jam with them. You probably can't pronounce their surnames, but who cares? They can't pronounce yours either, lol.

Today a lot of these bands bring in local musical elements into their compositions, which makes them distinctive and refreshing at the same time.

And you'll find albums by bands you've never heard or heard of. You'll find records of performances that you'll have to beat your heads to source in the West. Oh, yes, you will.

Here I assume some of you have been there or know about Shillong. Not surprising. Today it is known for when bands (which, between us, should have retired years earlier) visit the town when they are in India and, you'd say, because Meghalaya does not have the kind of militant activity which is constantly in the news, unlike Assam, Manipur and Nagaland. There are, of course, militant groups in Meghalaya, but they're small and don't do much.

One of the best things, and prolly very well-known,

about the Khasis and Garos is the importance of women in their societies. In these two tribes, the society is based around women, you see.

Which is where I got to explain a few things re matrilinear and other such definitions, but I'll make it short. They're kind of important, these distinctions, just so you'll know what makes these people what they are.

So. The Khasis, which are in central and mostly in eastern Meghalaya, are matrilinear and totally matriarchal. In the first case, Khasi families trace descent through their mothers, and their grandmothers before them. Inheritance and things like that are from mother to daughter only. And what about the sons, you'd ask? Ha, ha, they're married off, as people still do to daughters in other parts of the country. You'd think the more developed, as we say, places in India would have moved beyond such notions but they don't, which is sad.

Anyway, the Khasi boy marries into a family but he sure as heck knows he won't see a kopek of his wife's money, nor will his sons. That's matrilinear for you.

In the second case, the woman runs the family. She usually takes decisions on major matters and such, mostly without even consulting the husband, and she even has right of divorce, in which case the guy has to suck it up and kick himself for not being nice to her or whatever.

Garos, who live in the west, are matrilinear, same practice. But, and this is an important but, they are not matriarchal, that is, the family is sort of run jointly by the couple and so on.

Just in case you're beginning to imagine a total gender role reversal here in Meghalaya, hang on a sec. It's not like the husband sits at home and cooks and the wife goes to work or whatever wacky picture you might have in mind (which sort of implies that in other societies the wife stays home and cooks, which, imho, sucks equally. No one should stay at home, man, unless it is me and I have *World of Warcraft* on the Xbox . . . erm, never mind).

It is a reversal of position, of status, not of work as understood traditionally. The husband goes to work as well but because the wife runs the family the onus is more on her and plus, from what I've seen, the wife cooks at home too because most men are indifferent cooks no matter where they are born except those few guys with white cylindrical hats who don't count.

In effect, as you will have doubtless inferred already, the woman does housework and handles matters outside which means a double load of work, which, in the eyes of this champion slacker, is a very crummy state-of-affairs. So would I want to be a Khasi or Garo woman in that kind of society? Heck, no, but only because of that work bit.

What you end up arriving at after such a system being in place for like ages is some very strong, very, what's the word, resilient women. They are just at home at, erm, home, as they are out there in the cold. They are accustomed to being respected, they take their freedom as a given and return respect and freedom in equal measure, you just can't bend them no matter how much you try, they are cool and unflappable and used to solving problems, and they put in more sheer hard work per capita than the average plains*man*, all of which makes them very remarkable women. Not to put too fine a point on it, Khasi and Garo women are super-awesome.

Because, you know, life for the average person is difficult, in the hills. Sure, you and me, we are, at best, visitors. We go up in the hills, say the appropriate nice words with copious exclamation marks over a view or over a sunrise, we say how nice it would be to live here and so on, and then we return. But people who spend all their lives in such parts, even simple things are a big pain in every sense of the word. Take water, for instance, a problem we will meet again down in Nagaland in a bit. You see women from the slums in a big city, for instance, standing in queue at one of them water taps and carrying back bucketloads, day after day, that's hard. In the hills, because of an Italian called Torricelli, they have to work at merely pumping up the water and then carrying it up or downhill as the case may be. How many days can we do it, do you think, before we show the finger to the sunrise and return to the plains? Or think of carrying loads and bundles of things up an inclined road so narrow you can't take a car up it. Simple things, but difficult in so many different ways. So you got to admire women who handle all that, manage businesses very well, take care of the family and *still* are, at a very basic level, nice people.

So the last thing the Brits expected when they first arrived in these hills was such a social arrangement, and boy were they pissed. Not stopping to consider who was sitting on the throne back at home base, the later missionaries, who had occasion to journey much through the whole of Meghalaya and realised female dominance was not some kind of aberration but a very respected rule, they reacted. They jerked their psychological knees, in a manner of speaking.

In account after account by British administrators and missionaries, you will find phrases about 'the forward ways of these tribal women' and 'their brazen disregard for normal convention' which is another way of saying these were not societies where women played Fiddle Number 2. Man, it would have been a pleasure to see the expressions on these gents' faces just then.

You will also find repeated references to 'these scarlet-lipped women' or other phrases which imply that the women painted their lips in what must have been (for the visitors) an unseemly bright red. Man, it's a laugh. Betelnut. That's betelnut juice, what with the common custom throughout the North-east of chewing it, but here in Meghalaya the red lips became yet another bit of evidence about the morals of the women.

The weirdest part is, even accounts by Indians, who accompanied these Brits through Meghalaya, are along similar lines, from which you could say that—so far as chewing betelnuts goes, it being a familiar custom—these men were not very quick on the take. Or, alternately, were too eager to agree with the Brits' views.

Perhaps, you know, the plainsmen were reacting to the patriarchal notions they carried from their own societies. Whatever it was, they are very funny to read, these accounts. Shillong has a big archive with records going back to when it was the capital of undivided Assam, and if you happen to be in town and have some time on your hands, it is totally worth a visit, if you are prepared to look through the documents on your own.

All the strong-willed women of Meghalaya combined have, however, been unable to move, shake or even dent this one activity which takes up a lot of the time of a lot of slacker men and, actually, everyone else in this state.

This is about Shillong's city sport and Meghalaya's favourite one: no question about it at all, it is *teer*. To call it mere sport would, however, be such an unfair understatement that people familiar with it will take immediate umbrage, so I will call it what it really is. It is a passion. It is a social gathering, and it is probably the most respectable a gambling sport can get in any society. So you really do not want to rub a teer fan the wrong way, because of what it is.

Mainly it is bows and arrows. Say a particular number of archers, sometimes ten, sometimes more, are gathered at an equal set of targets, usually at a hundred and fifty yards. Within a fixed time, usually three minutes but could be longer, they have to shoot a hundred or more arrows at the targets, which are made of packed straw, rectangular in shape and about four feet in height, stuck on bamboo poles into the ground.

So you have these multiple arrows shot at them over a short time, the idea being to hit the targets and not so much where on the targets the hits are. Someone once actually showed me one of those XY-axis graphs with the frequency of hits, and, man, it is really a bell-shaped curve like they taught us in statistics class. At the beginning of this whooshing barrage, the archers are working up their rhythm and reach, so fewer arrows might hit. But the archers, being practiced, start hitting quickly and about the middle of the three minutes is when the most number of arrows find their mark. This frequency thing is of course totally irrelevant to the way the game is played but it goes to show that someone was crazy enough to do a statistical analysis in the hope, as he explained to me, that he could find a way of winning the game.

After the three minutes, the number of hits is counted. If, say, as in our example above, a thousand arrows are fired over this period, and 630 (an unusually low figure because the archers are good) find their mark, then the winning number is the last two digits, that is, 30. If you've put in money on this number for this shoot, you get twice your money back. In three minutes.

The person who thought this up must have had a really good day when he did, or was otherwise a remarkably subtle genius, because the game derives from the Khasis' and Garos' traditional and rather natural reliance on archery as a main offensive device. All the Khasi and Garo tribes have focused on archers in their armies, unlike other tribes of the region who opted for close-range weapons. Teer takes this passion and natural ability and adds to it the right degree of uncertainty on which every form of gamble depends. After all, gambling is not just a matter of simple probability, it is also a matter of random occurrences. You take a pack of 52 cards and derive countless kinds of games from it, all based on the chance of one card turning up instead of the other, and no way of accurately picking which one. Sure, you have very clever people who count cards in games like blackjack, but that can only get you so far, you know.

Teer is a bit like that. You have a thousand arrows, and the possibility of winning on any number from 00 to 99, but how, exactly, are you going to get it right? There are all the archers, and they do not shoot the same way, so where a few might be consistent, others might be having a bad day or a tic in the eyelid or something, and all the XY-axes and normal distribution curves in the world won't help you.

Unlike, say, the roulette table, teer is not based on a mechanical device (and thus the possibility of re-engineering it does not exist) but on purely human effort spread over large numbers, which adds to its attraction, is what I've been told on the few occasions I have attended a round or two.

That's the gamble, and people in Meghalaya are crazy about it. Some towns and big villages have like three or four rounds of contest per day; there is always a large crowd with tonnes of money in the pot. To my rather limited knowledge of the inner workings of the teer business, very very few people, if at all, have ever tried to throw or fix a game, or slipped a few to the, shall we say ... active players in the game, namely the archers. One reason for this is, like in the whole theoretical gambling scene I explained just now, there are so many archers that you can't get a fix on the winning number unless you get *all* the archers to work for you, and they have to work with one another in a miraculously telepathic way to make sure the total comes to your number because what if *one* of them gets it wrong?

I mean, consider the other sport where a lot depends on the human factor: horse-racing. As we all know from watching numerous heist movies of dubious provenance, one way to fix a race is to make the horse with the shortest odds lose, which is effected by either nobbling it or by having your lieutenant with the fake English accent and a wicked scar under his chin have a quiet word with the jockey on the evening before the race. In other words, bet against the odds and then pull the odds down. But in teer, it's a combination of man and double-digit number, so we have different levels of cutouts.

Besides, do you really want to tell an *archer*, to his face, without knowing if he is the conscientious type or not, that you want him to throw the game? Do you want to risk dissing a group of energetic young men who spend their waking hours putting sharp projectiles into targets? Go ahead, man. But try to make it to a round: the ambience and the crowd are very infectious.

Another reason, besides music, that some of you may be familiar with Shillong is from stories your grandparents might have told you, if they or *their* parents were with the Brit admin and were posted there. One nice posting it must have been: the quiet life, many places to travel within and out of town, excellent weather, good food, the works.

Anyway, one interesting offshoot of all these colonial postings is a lot of people who went on to do various things with their lives were born here. Arguably one of India's finest Shakespearian and otherwise actors, Utpal Dutt, was born here. So was Arundhati Roy (no, I will not make any smart comments here, so you, over there, don't even *dare* to throw that turnip. Yes, I can *see* it!).

Among all these people, one chap I'd particularly like you to remember while you go about your everyday life is John Shepherd-Barron, who was born here in 1925. No-no, he was Scottish, not English. Just remember him once in a while, alright? He invented the ATM.

About 55 kilometres south-east of Shillong is Cherrapunji

(*finally* a familiar name, applause all around. Sigh) and, next door, Mawsynram. Sadly, rains have decreased over the recent past in this part of the world, so the rainiest place in the world today is some bus-station something-or-the-other in Hawaii but, me friends, we will return, never fear.

There is more to Meghalaya besides these. West of Shillong, in the Garo Hills, is the big town of western Meghalaya, Tura. There are whole bunches of caves and lakes there, including these beautiful blue stalactite formations in the Siju Caves. Across a river near these caves is a bird sanctuary which you mustn't miss if you are there.

There are tonnes of waterfalls and lakes all over Meghalaya, and quite a few archaeological digs. You'll like these parts. By roads, in small towns and villages, you will get excellent food at great prices, to which you can value-add by catching hold of the local ancient citizen and getting a story or two out of him, about the old days.

Meghalaya is walkers' country. Between us, some of the places are best seen on a walk, so this place is like my second-favourite area to walk around in. No, I'm not telling you where the best place is. I found it after much effort etc. and its super-awesome, so it's my secret and likely to stay that way for some time because I have never met a fellow walker there, ever. Besides, it's in a different country.

There are trails up and down hills, the rises are negotiable, the vegetation . . . okay, alright, there is much undergrowth but what else can you expect in the one of the rainiest parts of the world? I mean, practically everything here is the 'wettest abc' or 'xyz'. Take Shillong Golf Course.

India's third-oldest, and the world's wettest, it's officially called the Gleneagles of the East. Yep. Officially. You'll do well with a humble mashie or two.

So, about walking. All you need to do is make sure you're kitted for rain and have functional footwear. But you knew that.

On these walks, you will find much to see, including great varieties of birds and simians.

Which reminds me: if you find yourself in the cave regions of central Meghalaya, do keep a sharp eye out. This is one of the last big pockets of the Indian sloth bear, which is very shy but, sloth or not, has huge fangs and rather long claws which at first are difficult to see because of the animal being very shaggy, so it is not exactly as cute as the Himalayan bear which, if you remember the dancing bears people used to drag around with a rope through their noses before the government stopped all that, was not as aggressive or untameable.

There used to be a time sloth bears were all over the subcontinent, you know. I've only seen one in the wild. One of the two animals I waited for a long time to see, the other being the firefox. I saw that one, didn't I? Yes, I did, but that's another story from elsewhere.

Ed.: You really should complete a story, you know.

SIX

In 1228 TSoC, a man called Chou-Lun Su-ka-pha came down to the plains of Assam from the east. As in other documented instances of someone journeying into a new land without a visa or quarantine certificates back then, Su-ka-pha did not travel alone: he had a whole frigging army with him, and he came to conquer and settle the place, which is considered a good option if you do not have a visa. Also, we cannot argue with this line of thought because if you are named Su-ka-pha, you are required by municipal law to carry a ten-kilo sword and command a few thousand men, at the very least, on a major campaign of conquest and expansion. For instance, whether or not you are familiar with a town called Carthage, based on your doubtless intimate knowledge of *Age of Empires II* you will know that when you say 'Hero Hannibal' there just *has* to be a mighty man sitting on a heavily armoured African elephant with golden tusks on your screen, after which, as an aside, I should mention that you'll type 'clear mist' and the other cheat codes and win handily. I'm just saying, man, I'm not actually accusing you of anything.

Ed.: Repeated references to somewhat obsolete strategy games can get on the nerves. Old Ahom saying.

Whatever, but some names just put a lot of moral pressure on their owners to be hardcore with or without edged implements and projectiles of varying lengths. Was reading a cracked.com article the other day about *The 9 Manliest Names in the World*, which featured Lance Armstrong, Powers Boothe, Stirling Mortlock and Max Planck and No.1 (deservedly) was Sgt Max Fightmaster, a name which is simply impossible to believe actually exists in this here mundane world, but there it is.

Su-ka-pha, blessed with such a triple-plated name, however did not have the advantage of cheat codes and had to do a lot of legwork before reaching level 14. He was a Tai-Shan, a branch of a northern Burmese tribe which we shall meet again later in our travels here. The Tai-Shan are connected with the Thais and other ethnic groups in this part of the world, and possibly even with Quin Shi Huang Ti, who as we know was the first real Chinese emperor and gave that country his name.

Su-ka-pha (the Chou-lun part of his name is an honorific meaning 'prince' or some such) had taken leave of his brother, the king in northern Burma, and had come away with about 9,000 followers to see what could be done on the other side of the Patkai Range. His men and their descendants became known as the Tai-Ahoms or Ahoms. There is an old story about the founding of the kingdom that we all hear at our grandmothers' knees. Considering those times, it is a likely story.

It is said that Su-ka-pha and his men crossed first into the Naga Hills through the Patkai Mountains from Burma. Here they were met in battle by an all-tribes Naga contingent. The Ahoms defeated and captured the chiefs. Later they invited the remaining Naga chiefs in the hills to a dialogue. The captured chiefs were cooked and served to the 'guest' chiefs.

The Nagas signed a deal and let the invaders through into the Brahmaputra Valley.

The story reminds me of Kaiser Soze from *The Usual Suspects*, specifically that part where he had a little fracas with a bunch of Hungarian mobsters and took certain ... specific measures. I suppose it is all about the will to do whatever is necessary at a particular time to fulfil an operational requirement. I don't think men in such stories ever said: 'Oh God, I am so sorry, the other guy made me do it' or 'But wait, you should understand the circumstances behind the deed, I am not usually such a person, you know' or other kinds of moralising or amateur psychology which might make it a p.c. news item. I suppose all they would say is 'It had to be done, so I did it. It doesn't matter thinking about what if it had been otherwise. It wasn't.'

Am I getting ahead of the story here or something? I see you're scratching your heads and wondering where this history primer and R-rated action suddenly sprang out at you from. We're going to east Assam. Remember what it is called there? Oh, alright, go back to the earlier chapter. Go on, I'll wait.

Got it? Great. Shall we go on, then?

We're going to east Assam, and to understand the place you've got to understand the last eight hundred years, or how the Assamese people, as we know them today, were formed. But I'll go easy on the history if you want.

The short version, then, is Su-ka-pha, on reaching the valley, knew in his heart that he didn't want to go further and commenced to found his kingdom. We do not criticise his decision because the first sight of the valley from the Naga Hills is beyond breathtaking.

This empire-building is not an easy task, and Su-ka-pha and his descendents had to take down, one after the other, all the old kingdoms, alliances and tribal republics that had been here since the days of Bhaskar Varman. Where possible, the Ahoms brought the people under direct control. Where terrain interfered, such as in today's Nagaland, a few tributes and appropriate words were enough.

Assamese society as we know it today, took shape under the Ahoms. Over the centuries, the Ahoms took in the Hinduism of the valley and gave back stability, a fierce territorial pride and a shift away from the rest of the country, which you have to understand if you have ever asked why in Assam, which has the same religion and a similar language, there has been such a fertile ground for separatism.

You see, before the Ahoms, although Assam hadn't been under various Indian empires, there had been a lot of fraternising, as I've mentioned earlier, what with foreign visitors dropping in for the odd chat once in a while. But the Ahoms, in the six hundred continuous years they ruled over the land they loved from the moment they set foot on it and which they called The Golden Casket, they were plain about this: the land does not belong to anyone else so just stay away. Trade and other things: good. Cultural exchange, religious preachers coming and going: very nice. Technology: keep sending. Expansion: umm, no, sorry.

There were a few palace coups, a deal of intrigue, treason and whatnot which livened things up sometimes, but you cannot have such a continuous period of political stability without a lot of civilisational progress and some very strong national identity.

Imho, the Ahoms notched up two very significant contributions which make these six hundred years important for any student of human society. Point the first: they had a fanatical regard for history and records, an almost obsessive compulsion to put in words everything that happened with them. So, practically from the moment Su-ka-pha reached the valley, his men began compiling the Great Chronicles of Assam. These were known as *buronji* which translates as 'a library to explain things to functionally retarded people' or something along those lines. Everything they found went into it, by which I mean everything: revenue records, cultivation figures and agricultural productivity, the names and descriptions of animals and plants, climate patterns, administrative hierarchies, the works. It was a cross between a closed-source Wikipedia and classified CIA documents. And they *kept at it* for the next six centuries.

These documents were available to the public for reference, particularly in case of disputes, such as if someone accused you of infra-dig parentage, you could go to the buronji-sensei (who I imagine to be a somewhat young-looking Pai Mei) and demand to be shown your family records and prove your case.

The accuracy of the buronjis were their undoing: in the early nineteenth century, some high official, doubtless a paranoid fellow, suspecting that the records would prove him of lower birth, vandalised large parts of the archives, which must have been a task because a lot of them were on copper-plate.

By the fifteenth century, the Ahom kingdom had expanded to cover the whole of the valley, with a lot of client states in the hills, and things looked good. A hundred years later, the Mughal expansion began, and the Mughals, as we know, were not easy to stop. Sometime around the early seventeenth came the second-biggest innovation of the Ahoms that would stop the Mughals: the *paik* system.

Y'see, there were in medieval times just two kinds of military-administrative systems. One was feudal, with knights, barons and such, best seen in Western continental Europe and the British Isles, a pyramidal structure where the only professional soldiers were the knights, while the bulk of the army was made of conscript—and therefore poorly trained and inadequately armed—peasants. The other was the samurai system which was differently structured, being also a pyramid, but limited to the warrior class and therefore unable to tap the vast population of farmers.

Paik comes under neither system. The man who founded it was also the governor of the eastern provinces and his idea was to militarise *all* citizens, thus working around the whole low-population problem, and have a large army, just in case. So neighbours were set up into little groups of four each, one male per family. This unit would practise together with weapons and other military stuff and was the basic unit, ready to be called up very quickly when required by their country.

Ten such units would be under a military-admin chap called a Bora, a hundred under a Saikia, a thousand under a Hazarika, 5,000 under a Rajkhowa and such. This singular system not only led to a well-trained standing army, but also a very scientific way to administer the country. *And* now you know a bit about some Assamese surnames. (Knowledge Plus: Borgohains and other Gohains were ministers, Phukans were like three star general-ranked people and so on.)

Momai Tamuli Borborua, who thought this up, as well as other administrative reform thingies, was just on time because the Mughals began a series of rather large invasions into the valley in the seventeenth cent. The paik system was the chief reason the Assamese could take the heavy punishment and casualities that inevitably came during the invasion. But Momai Tamuli need not have worried about the leadership of these men because he had a son who would become even more legendary than him. His name was Lachit.

In the 1660s, when Lachit was made the *borphukan* (governor) of Guwahati and the western provinces, the new king's directions to him were simple: the Mughals have occupied large parts of our land (in fact this one time they'd even reached the capital, deep in east Assam). See them off, will you? Lachit said he would.

By this time, as you know, the Mughals were a hundred years in power and had another forty to go, but they were in their prime, and got in a huge land army and an equally impressive navy from Dhaka to take out the last free kingdom in the east. There were soldiers from almost every part of the Mughal empire which has resulted in some comparisons of what happened subsequently with Thermopylae but this is somewhat inaccurate because, remember, in T. the Greeks *lost*. Plus it wasn't one epic battle here but a series of skirmishes, raids and at least one disastrous cavalry charge by the Ahoms in which 12,000 heavy cavalrymen were blown to bits by Mughal artillery, one of the biggest single casualty figures in the whole history of the kingdom.

You know, I keep talking about Lachit and yes, he's a personal hero but there is a solid reason for that. He was a genius at what he did, popular with his troops (which not every good general can say about himself), knew how to handle political pressures from his royal bosses and loved his land.

He also knew his land, so on mapping the hills around Guwahati, he made what Blackadder's sidekick Baldrick would call 'a cunning plan'. He designed a set of artificial hills connecting the real hill ranges to one another (y'see, there are two hill ranges on both banks of the river at this point). From behind these fortifications, his men played out a waiting game and made little guerilla raids on the Mughal infantry.

The invaders, hemmed in on land and sick from the diseases and fever the swamps contributed, took to the river on their big ships, but Lachit was ready for this all along. He took the smaller, more agile boats of his navy, encircled the big slow invader ships and won the day. The few who escaped what we know today as the Battle of Saraighat in 1671 limped into Dhaka and stayed there for the next eight years.

Lachit, who was dying of blood poisoning during the battle, did not make it back to the Ahom capital of Garhgaon, but his army did, carrying his body. There they discovered that some idiot minister, taking advantage of those suspense-filled days in the kingdom, had deposed the king and was seated on the throne smirking away into his beard (which I doubt he had because Ahoms did not go in much for facial hair).

It happens thus, far too often. The poor soldiers are away fighting for their lands and people or some abstract but strong idea, and at home some civilian or rear-echelon type hops-skips-and-jumps to power or otherwise subverts the very system and state the soldiers are fighting for.

It happened once in the US, you know, and I must tell you this story because it, like Saraighat and its aftermath, are illustrative of the moral that you must really not go out of your way to piss off war heroes to whom you owe a deal more than you suspect.

In Arkansas, there is a town called Hot Springs, which started as a health resort kind of place but gradually became the vice capital of the country round about 1945. That year, victorious Arkansas armymen returned from Europe to find that the mob had taken over the town, the mayor, the district attorney, hotels, casinos, nightclubs and perhaps even the Janitor's Union and the town was the most corrupt in the country.

The GIs got a hardcore district attorney elected, went to the mob boss who was ruling Hot Springs and told him something similar to what the evil-looking senator tells Howard Hughes in *The Aviator*: 'We just defeated Germany and Japan. Who the hell are you?'

The GIs ran the mob out of Hot Springs in what is now known as the GI Revolt, a classic crime-fighting story if ever there was one. (A sidelight is this cleanup led to the mob relocating their casinos and such to a small town in the Nevada Desert called Las Vegas.)

The veterans of Saraighat, therefore, found that while they had been fighting and dying like flies in the rain for ten years, their country had quietly gone to the dogs under a usurper who might or might not have had a beard but definitely had no claims to the throne.

Lachit's men, who had not yet buried their general, followed the universal custom in such situations, and went berserk. They just marched into Garhgaon, contrary to the usual rules that a full army never camped at the capital, told the guards and such to stay away if they knew what was good for them, walked into the throne room, picked up the evil minister-fellow and threw him out, making sure he landed on something sharp and, preferably, rusted. Then they brought the rightful king back to the throne, gave a final pump-up speech to the ministers and nobles to rule the country wisely and well because *they would be watching*, gave Lachit a state funeral and returned to their villages.

The Ahoms used to build great earthen burial mounds or *moidam* for their big guys, which over the years would be overgrown with grass and look like Rohirrim graveyards. I went to Lachit's moidam, near Jorhat. Under disrepair after the end of the kingdom, it is a neat little place today. The Corps of Engineers and local citizens contributed to building a beautiful park and arch here, with two cannons (called *bortop*) and the general's statue. Sadly, on all the occasions that I have visited the place, there seemed to be very few visitors, so anyone passing that way, do drop in, it's only a kilometer from the Assam Trunk Road.

Amar Chitra Katha, which for my generation used to be *the* source for Indian mythology and history, and told so much better than the textbooks, had an issue on Lachit once, I remember. I think it showed him as a tall, slim and dashing young guy with a pencil moustache and all. The larger-than-lifesize statue at his moidam is probably more authentic and shows a sturdily-built man of average height and with a remarkably angry expression on his face, which might actually be closer to the truth. I think it would have to be a very focused person to pull off what he did. Medieval armies and administrative units were hardly easy to control and direct, what with communication hassles and slow transport, so it would need a forceful person who could summon, when needed, the Incredible Hulk inside him if things got bad, instead of cultivating a serene expression and a set of devastating one-liners like a Brit general in a 1960s war movie, the one-liners delivered deadpan. So, yes, he was perhaps angry.

But I believe Lachit was actually angry because he, like other great men before and after him, was saddled with the most nefarious, conniving and generally asinine set of relations one can imagine. In fact, I believe that apart from his father, who as we have seen was a great man, there were very few male members that Lachit could with dignity claim kinship with, which might have something to do with the possibility that between *pere et fils*, the two men had inadvertently soaked in all the awesomeness a family can legally possess at any single moment in history, thus leaving the rest floundering in the gene pool without a suitable floatation device.

For e.g.: his mother's brother, whose name I do not remember at the moment due to a very justifiable *damnatio memoriae*, but that's okay because his was a serious instance of lead poisoning in the brain cells when a child. At Guwahati, while constructing his artificial hills, Lachit wanted the job done quickly so his men could be ready for the invaders who were on their way upriver any moment. So he assigned a key section of the building work to his uncle and told him to get his men to hop to it.

The next morning, after another night of working hard

with his men digging up earth and muddy to his eyebrows, Lachit did a tour of work progress and came upon his uncle peacefully and happily snoring on the hillside, the job woefully incomplete.

Pressed for time and thus denied a large bit of movie-chewing dialogue and energetic arguments, Lachit delivered a snappy line to the effect that his mother's brother was not more important than his country and got his uncle executed.

This was not the end of the depraved depths to which his relations were to reach. Eight years after Saraighat, Lachit's brother, who became governor of the western provinces after the general died, sold the fort at Guwahati to the Mughals and ran off. It took another war-filled decade or so to undo this crippling blow.

Meanwhile, some of the Boys have remarked that a man leading an *Assamese* army into a battle for survival would end up more than slightly pissed off with his troops, but that is typical Assamese self-deprecation so I urge you not to pay much attention to that sort of remark.

You see, the oh-so-completely cliched concept of *lahe-lahe* (slowly, slowly) is, some Assamese claim, what defines us today: an easygoing people perennially in the comfortable armchair of life. This one time at a seminar in Delhi, one of my editors, who once worked as a correspondent in Assam and is a Punjabi, told the crowd that 'The Assamese are so easygoing, they make Bengalis look like Punjabis.' My friend G. (with whom I had, if you remember, the conversation about the swamps of Guwahati) once had a conversation with a Keralite friend about cultural traits. You know the old joke: one Mallu, coconut oil factory, two

Mallus, a communist party, three Mallus, a Gulf emigration agency, and such. On being asked what the similar count for Assamese was, G. came up with this gem, which I was present as an occasional Boswell to record: one Assamese, slumber party, two Assamese, slumber party, three Assamese, *big* slumber party.

Erm, any Assamese in the crowd (I can spot a few getting agitated), I'll give you G.'s number if you want to have a quiet word with him. I would give it this instant, but first I shall take a nap.

We might or might not be laidback today, but back then things were up and happening. Lazy people in the kingdom were particularly targeted and there was in fact a highway which was constructed by all the lazy people the king once rounded up and put to work. I swear there was this highway and it was called *Dhudor Ali*: The Highway of Lazy People, although the translated term does not have the same ring to it as the word *dhud* has.

As another sidelight, the Ahoms, though never a majority, contributed to the modern Assamese language with many words which have absolutely no Sanskrit roots and are therefore utterly incomprehensible to people who know similar languages, such as Bengali. There. That's a little secret I just told you.

In the nineteenth cent the kingdom was a little weakened by internal problems when the second big invasion took place, this time from the east. The kingdom of Ava in central Burma had defeated Manipur and was on its way into the Brahmaputra valley. It swept aside the Ahom army in one brutally-fought engagement after the other, destroyed the capital Mongol-style, and killed more than one-third of the men in the valley. This was the darkest period of Assam's history, a time which came to be infamous as *Maanor Din*: 'the days of the Maan', as the Burmese were called. The kingdom was destroyed, the people weakened, and in 1828, the Brits walked in.

The second bridge across the Brahmaputra is at a place called Koliabor, 150 km east of Guwahati, where the first bridge is. The area east of Koliabor is Upper Assam and has been so for hundreds of years. Upper Assam was the heart of the kingdom, and eastward of Koliabor are the towns of Golaghat, Jorhat, Sivasagar, Dibrugarh and Tinsukia, successively.

The ISBT I described back in Guwahati has a row of different night buses you can catch for Upper Assam. One of the good things (and there are a lot of them) about a bus trip in Assam is the bus network nomenclature. Most bus services in other parts of the country are named after gods and things, which while impressive in some cases, are not exactly peaceful-sounding, which you'd think would be the first criterion for making passengers feel at ease. If you were to travel in Gujarat, it will appear that you have two options: Srinath Travels and Srinathji Travels. While this great difference is laudable, it is also prosaic, because you feel like you are traveling in a bus owned by a former Indian medium pacer. Also, possibly the only logical response when you see Srinath Travels is 'Good for him.'

Ed.: Yeah, right, I can see the readers cracking up.

In Karnataka, particularly its north, people are big fans of the Chalukyas. This is not surprising, seeing as the whole place was under that dynasty at some point. So you have

Chalukya Travels. Makes you feel you're on a campaign somewhere and should be carrying triangular flags or such.

Assam has Green Valley and Blue Hills Travels. I do not exactly know which one came first because they have been around since before me, but it is likely that one or the other, being second in line, took the 'colour-first-name-geography-second-name' system and kept at it. Any way you consider it, they are very nice names for bus services, as is Sylvan Dee, which, you clever people will instantly notice, is an exact synonym for Green Valley. Red River, which could be another way of describing the valley, has not been tried at the time of going to press and might not have the same ring to it but in these degenerate times, who knows? I can only say that I will *not* get on a bus which says Red River Travels.

Cabs and such are also available for hire from Guwahati to any part of Assam.

The journey is comfortable, the roads are smooth and there is a lot to see as you go by. Principally, to the south, you will see the hills of Meghalaya rising near the horizon, and to the north a stretch of green fields, ponds and villages.

A road trip in the valley is incomplete without stopping at any of the several restaurants, where the food is uniformly good. I have never eaten at a highway restaurant where the food has not been good, so I can vouch for them. The best place to stop at is Jokholabondha where, since most private cars and buses stop anyway, the prices are good, and there might even be a few places where, apart form the usual chicken-fish-mutton *thalis* you might also get pigeon or, in this one place I must have hit by pure magnificent chance one time, duck. Curry is made the right way (or what I think is the right way, you might not), so is the rice, and service, as far as I have seen, swift.

Assamese is one of the few surviving major languages of the world in which the first written work was not epic poetry, but prose. Icelandic, if I remember correctly, is among the others. The Upper Assamese dialectical variant of the tongue is beautiful, refined and full of courtesy. Even a very angry Upper Assamese does not sound too rough, provided he does not swear too much.

The land from Golaghat eastwards is a plain stretch from the south bank of the river to the Naga Hills. Golaghat also has Kaziranga, so you will probably visit it anyway. This is at a point where a spur of the Naga Hills moves westward towards the river. This spur, which the highway to Upper Assam crosses, is called Burha Pahar or Old Mountain. Was a time the name made people tense and gitchy while travelling. Back in the Eighties, when the highway left much to be desired and the road was one hairpin bend after the other, someone would whisper to the driver: 'We've reached Burha Pahar, drive slowly', and the car's occupants would seize up and concentrate, as if by willing it they could *make* the car safe. There was practically not an alternate day without a big accident on this mountain, and even today, when the highway is broad and reasonably safe, people wake up in the middle of the night when they cross Old Mountain.

It is particularly sticky in winters, when the mist is thick over the road, and elephants cross into the corridors of the reserved forest on either side. Aside from Kaziranga, where you can obviously expect to see elephants, Assam has seen a recent surge in what can only be called the 'unemployed elephants issue'. This has to do with a ban, some years back, on cutting forest timber. While the timber mafia has, with the ingenuity typical of self-respecting mafias elsewhere, shrugged off the ban and carried on, the only casualty has been the elephants that were used to cart the logs back in the day. In short, the elephant, like the batchloads of engineers of various specialisations Assam continues to produce by the year, and who *still* expect government jobs in the days of Guwahati Shining, is unemployed.

Now, discerning listener that you are, you will ask here what connection an elephant might have with an engineer, and indeed, apart from the fact that they are unemployed and unemployable under the current scheme of things, you are correct. But whereas an engineer might conceivably be funded by his long-suffering parents until such time as a suitable job emerges, an elephant cannot be, principally because it eats a lot, compared to an engineer who, being a nerd, might actually have a small appetite.

So these mighty mammals are either turned loose in the forests from where they return periodically on daring raids with their wild cousins, or, in collaboration with their equally jobless mahouts wait along roadsides to mug off-roaders and other such heavy vehicles which, if you look at it, are the only reasonable match for such a formidable mugger (is that the right word?). In short, if you are in a small vehicle (by which I mean anything less well-endowed than an AMX-30) and are stopped on a highway by an unemployed elephant, pay up, dude, in cash or bananas. There are upwards of 1,500 such unemployed elephants in Assam, most of whom, I am relieved to report, are not in the mugging business.

I love Jorhat. It is such a neat little town, with clean roads and nice little houses, drains that actually drain. I hope the look lasts, and it might because this, the last capital of the kingdom, has survived beautiful and intact through the Raj, the glory days of Shillong and today's shift in political power centres westward. In fact Jorhat has actually looked better and better over the years. The story of the kingdom is not, in case you've been thinking, just one chapter after another of violence. North and east of Jorhat is Majuli, the world's largest river island. At least it used to be before erosion set in. Floods in Assam have been particularly bad after the 1950 earthquake, which was so big it pushed the riverbed up. Since then, the river has flooded every year in increasing arcs, and torn out vast areas of the banks. There are many people you might meet whose ancestral homes were along the riverbank and which have since been washed away.

I do not know how much land has been lost to the river in Majuli, but it is substantial. The island is dotted with *xatras*, places of Vaishnavite worship, literature and cultural explorations, and if for nothing else, Majuli needs to be preserved for these houses alone, some of which are precariously close to the riverbank which has been eating away steadily, and might take them off next year, or the year after that. The great preacher and reformer Srimanta Sankardev set these places up across the valley in the thirteenth and fourteenth centuries. Some of you must have seen Xattriya dance performances.

Sivasagar was the capital for some time, and the other capital, Garhgaon, was at a place off the Assam Trunk Road and just a short distance from Sivasagar. The Rang

Ghar and the Kareng Ghar, the two most-recognisable monuments of the Ahom kingdom, are here. They are not buildings in the same way as other places we recognise as monuments usually are, but that has to do with their traditional function.

The Kareng Ghar is in Garhgaon and about a 15-kilometre drive from Sivasagar town. It was the royal complex from the early fifteenth to the eighteenth cent, so when they started building it and the fortified town around it, it must have been of timber. Now, good quality timber it must have been, but wood nevertheless, so it did not last, except the fort wall which they wisely made of brick, thus giving the place its name, which means the Fort Village, translating literally. In the eighteenth cent, the royal palace was replaced with a brick structure. It is four storeys tall, with each successive floor smaller as you go up. The fourth floor is topped with a dome. There are watchtowers and things on it and the place could double up as the secret residence of a major sorcerer or someone, because those places, as we know, are a bit crumbly and so is this one.

In the days of the kingdom, the Rang Ghar, which is *very* near Sivasagar, used to be a pavilion, two storeys high, from where the king and his court could observe sports and festivals which took place in front of them.

The first time you see Rang Ghar will not be before someone has filled you in that it's also a symbol of the golden age, so you will have different associations going on in your head when you stand in front of it (there's a nice walkway leading up to it and grassy lawns on either side), but you will note that it is shaped, were the roof to be taken off, like an octagon. However, the centre of this is a rectangular room with wings going out from its sides, fronted by curved doors. The roof is a gentle slope, a parabola I think you'd call it. The doors were built that way mainly for the view during those games and contests I talked about. If you are the kind who looks very closely at the walls and carvings on old buildings, you'll see what look like small broken bits of rice on the walls here, as in the other buildings. Or you will see them if you have been told to look out for them. The thing is, these structures were held together by a mix of a kind of rice and limestone, an earlier version of cement. This mix is remarkably strong and was used to plaster the walls as well.

Rang Ghar is not just some place where the king used to have a little R&R. Having a kingdom is one thing, building a culture is another. Having these games and stuff gave a certain character to the people and sent out a message, you see: we are secure and we can take some time off from (take your pick) wars, conquests, famines and stuff and have a good time, seeing as these games, including buffalo fights, martial displays and all were hugely popular among the people. And *that's* why a mere games pavilion is rated over the main palace complex of Talatal Ghar, a handy pebble's flick away.

This is also why the ULFA was formed here back in the spring of 1979, by these half-dozen guys.

That year was a watershed for the state and the people. The anti-illegal migrants campaign, led by student activists, was at its peak. People had begun to question, once again, that niggle of doubt that had never gone out in the valley since 1962: was it okay to continue with a state that was not looking out for its people? What was the solution to this? More important, what was the *new* solution to this, because the party then in power was the same one which led Assam through the bad ole days of Partition when a large part of the state nearly got packed to East Pakistan?

Those guys at the Rang Ghar thought they had a solution: armed rebellion. So the ULFA was formed, and truth is, it was very popular when it started. Those who did not entirely buy into the independent socialist Assam theory at least went with the idea that this was a new method of making a people heard in Delhi. You can argue about the methods on and off, but there's no denying the ULFA's humungous popular base back then.

It went out quickly, though. Unlike, say, the Naga rebels, the ULFA targeted local people much more frequently, did not take as much time in leaving the lines of communication open with the public, things like that. In their defence, it could be said that the Naga rebels (who we will meet shortly) had a lot of time to unite the people behind their actions. The ULFA, on the other hand, had to do things quickly.

And, man, did they mess up. They got into the extortion game like *that*, you know, serving notices like all over the place, abductions, killings, what have you. Eleven years later the Army launched operations under President's Rule, the leaders went underground, the men went into neighbouring countries.

It has been a fairly steady slide since then, with reports every now and then of how much money the organisation has been making in hotels, businesses, hospitals and such in Bangladesh and elsewhere. Lately, its operational ability like totally wiped out, the ULFA has taken to blaming the people for its failures, which is totally unfair, but who's to tell them. And, man, killing children, that's the tops. That's effing it.

Never mind them. There are some very interesting places remaining to be seen here in Sivasagar so we better return to it.

Ordinary houses in Assam, back till just a while back, were of mud and lightweight material, designed to survive things like 1854, 1897 and 1950 but not, alas, time.

But Sivasagar, which you absolutely must visit if you are in Upper Assam, has, within an arc of about a dozen kilometres, the complete architectural history of Assam's golden age. About three kilometres from Sivasagar town is the Talatal Ghar, which used to be the main palace complex of the kings for about three hundred years, which means there was a good deal of building and renovation here. You will find palaces, barracks, trading posts, all the works a medieval town used to have. You will, however, be a little surprised that the scale of these buildings does not match the scale or duration of the kingdom. You'll be thinking, as you see the carvings and stuff on the walls and the unique spires on the palaces, that a kingdom as stable as the Ahoms' could have had big palaces. But the builders had to push the envelope only as far as the earthquakes permitted, so they were clever that way, seeing as the Talatal Ghar complex survives, though a little scratched here and there by the long claws of time.

Eww, was that a flowery sentence? I detest flowery sentences, man. I see an f.s., I break out in seven different and unclassifiable kinds of sweat. I get verbal spring fever.

I did it again, didn't I? It's an epidemic, man.

There are a lot of other buildings and structures too that you could take a look at, including the stone bridge of Namdang, built at a time of mainly horse travel, because carriages were not really a good idea and were slowed in the mud of the rains. Carriage travel never took off in the kingdom, so the stone bridge of Namdang looks far too strong for just horses, but there you have it. The Assam Trunk Road, on its way east from Sivasagar, passes over another masonry bridge built by the Ahoms and which now has the highway going over it, so how is that for permanence?

Sivasagar is called thusly because it is a hub or centre of Shaivite worship. Once the Ahoms had got the whole kingdom thing going, they assimilated rather rapidly and picked up Hinduism, version 0.1 (Shiva worship) and 0.2 (Vishnu worship) and took to it with the fanaticism of the new convert. Of course, it was also a trickle-down kind of thing, so it was only after a succession of Hindu Ahom kings that the nobility and priests were into it en masse.

Temple-building was the next stage, *au naturel*. Little before the middle of the eighteenth, after a few practice specimens here and there in the valley, the then queen built the Shiva Dole, which could be one of the tallest Shiva temples in the world. It could actually be *the* tallest because it stands about 55 metres in its socks and is nearly 60 metres in diameter. On its top you will see this big cap of gold (a *kalasha* is what the historian is heard saying, is it?) which the Burmese, in their all-out campaign, appear to have missed. That there cap itself is about two metres high although it could be taller because this is only what I have been told and I have had no means of what you people love to call empirical verification but from the ground it looks about that size so we'll let it pass.

Next to it are the two other temples of the complex, for Vishnu and the Mother Goddess, so you have basically all three big sects of the religion side by side, and it is a pretty sight. You will not be missing the Shiva Dole because you can see it from everywhere in Sivasagar, discounting the hoardings which, each time I visit, seem to have been multiplying like lemmings.

Next to this complex is the lake which gives the town its name. Sivasagar Lake was built totally by hand along with the temples for the whole temple-dip routine and till just a decade or so ago, used to be clean like nothing else but got plasticked kind of unmercifully in the middle before local citizens did things on their own, although there is a bit remaining to be done.

You could also visit the Joy Temple (the word coming from 'victory', not 'happiness', before you ask) and the Joy Lake next to it. This is the largest man-made water storage tank ever made, though why everyone keeps calling it a tank I do not understand because it is like more than three hundred *acres* in area and is nearly three hundred years old, giving it awesomeness in the twin areas of size and age. It is usually full and brimming but again, like Sivasagar Lake, it has got a bit plasticked which is a terrible shame.

But on any given day there are remarkably few visitors to either spot, considering this is such a major temple area, so both places are generally peaceful lakes to sit by and think about whatever may occur to you at the moment.

SEVEN

Dibrugarh, due east of Sivasagar, is another old town and used to be an important part of the kingdom. Today it is Assam's third-largest town after Guwahati and Jorhat, and the state's version of Atlantis.

Back before 1950, Dibrugarh was a major port and prosperous trading town, at the meeting of the valley and the mountains of east Arunachal and Nagaland. It had what were among the best-made houses in Assam, and among the most cultured folk, with a lot of theatre and other activities.

Then Medog came calling and left a sucker-punch of a visiting card. The big houses, theatres and factories were levelled by the temblor. Most of the residences and shops back then were next to the river, just as people build houses near highways today.

Then the riverbed got pushed up and the worst floods the valley had ever seen swept into the first of the big towns on the plain. More than three-fourths of the town got washed away. Today, underneath the southern arc of the river around Dibrugarh lie the submerged areas. Perhaps someday the river will change its course and we'll see them again.

Dibrugarh took its time recovering from this biblical event, but the town had lost much of what made it such a wonderful place. Except the people, that is. With Jorhat, Dibrugarh ranks right up there for having produced some of the nicest people in the entire valley, as well as some really good students. The schools and colleges of this area have traditionally been alma maters for Assam's famous administrators, teachers and other such important people.

Part of its economic might was, however, taken away by Tinsukia, a relatively new town on an ancient land. Tinsukia, the transport capital of Upper Assam and just a short distance east of Dibrugarh, is on land that once belonged to the Motok people, the kingdom the Ahoms rolled over first to begin their expansion. As history caught up with this place, it kind of kept a tenuous hold on Assam's economy, being within the tea belt. But after Medog, Tinsukia became a powerhouse, mainly in trucking. But it takes more than that to build a proper town.

They say tea was first discovered in China. But there is a text or two in Chinese (which I have heard of from reliable folks but have not read) which rather categorically say that the plant was first introduced into China by this Chinese Buddhist monk who'd taken it from here during his travels in search of Buddhist texts in the third cent. These Chinese monk-dudes were all over the place looking for texts, weren't they?

The Japanese, however, say this wasn't no Chinese monk at all but an Indian who'd gone to China. Dunno who this guy was, prolly the same monk who founded the Shaolin Temple or the other guy who invented Shaolin boxing. It is however, interesting, the difference between the Chinese and Japanese versions. How d'you mix up between a Chinese and an Indian monk, eh? Mysterious, highly mysterious.

The point is, there used to be a tea plant totally native

to Assam. Tribes like the Khamti in Arunachal have been drinking tea for at least eight hundred years, they say categorically.

Moving away from surmises and such, the stuff you call 'Assam tea' is not, strictly speaking, from Assam. I have not yet found a strain of the old, genuine, species of the plant which grew in Assam before the Brits came. Maybe in some forest somewhere the species still exists. I haven't seen it, thassall.

What you, on the other hand, now know as Assam tea is a hybrid of this old species and Chinese tea which the Brits brought in. So if you combine the Chinese texts with Assam's history from the 1830s, you get Chinese tea, a descendent itself of Indian tea, hybridising with the original species.

So, back in the 1830s, the Brits were making their inroads into the Assam Valley which they'd treatied off the Burmese, when they came across Khamti and Singpho tribesmen merrily brewing the same plant they'd been buying off China. So the Brits created a hybrid from these two species and began clearing off suitable land to grow it on their own and thus show the finger to the Chinese. By the late 1830s, the tea industry was on its way.

They would eventually set up estates across the Assam Valley and today there are estates even in Karbi Anglong and the Barak Valley. But for quality, production volume, soil fertility and suitable rainfall, they found Upper Assam an ideal tea land. This is where the hills roll to a halt in undulating gradients, so rain kind of flows away after watering the tea plants and such and this, y'see, is exactly what they need—not too much, not too little, good soil and the right amount of sun and shade, which is why you have all those big trees between the plants. Fussy plants they are, and if allowed to grow can become ginormous. Chances are, if you pass a full-grown tea plant in the wild, you might not be able to recognise it because it grows upwards of eight feet. The trimming and flat-top routine is so the topmost buds and leaves can be harvested.

The first landfall of Britified tea cultivation was at a place called Chabua, about 25 km from Dibrugarh, which is why the area around it is almost completely tea country today. You can guess how much clout this plant would eventually command when I tell you Chabua means 'Tea Sown' in Assamese, so it either means someone ran out of inspiration or the place became a legend very quickly. Guess.

But merely clearing large swathes of forest land was not the whole story of tea. The Brits had to do some old-style demographic shifts to get the manpower that went along with creating a new industry in a new land. The old expedient (that the right word?) of getting bunches of Indians with various fake promises on board ships for sugar plantations on malarial islands in the Caribbean had to be customised in a different way.

At first they tried the Khamtis and Singphos as labour, picking and processing the leaves, on the excellent—if I may say so—idea that people who'd been brewing a better-tasting tea than the Chinese for at least a thousand years would know everything there was to know about tending the plants.

Here the Brits erred, magnificently. For the Ks and Ss had been perfectly content picking off wild tea leaves and making the brew as a lark, just enjoying the dadgum thing for the heck of it. All that processing, packaging, marketing and the rest were, they thought, spoiling the fun, and I don't blame them. So the Ks and Ss said if the Brits wanted to make money off their plant, they'd have to pay them decent wages, at least. (Here I should remind you that the Singphos were among the first people to rebel against the Brits in the 1830s, practically the moment they stepped into the region, so they could be stubborn and didn't care much for these new rulers).

Having said their piece, they went back to their villages, leaving the new industry and the Brits floundering in mid-tide. At this point they were about to give up the experiment, but remembered just in time that there were like masses of unorganised tribals in central India who could be given the old carrot-and-stick and brought in as labour.

Thus began India's biggest economic transmigration, and, till the Partition, the largest forced movement within the subcontinent of a people from their land. Santhals, Bhils and what-have-you, they were loaded on transport of various kind and shipped from the Chhotanagpur region, mainly to Upper Assam. The tea industry took off and has never looked back since.

These people today form an entirely distinctive group in Assam and are known as the Tea Tribes, their language a patois of their native tongues and Assamese. They have no connection with where they came from or who they used to be, and for a long time they had access to the barest living conditions, just enough healthcare to get them on their feet and back to picking, no education and non-existent political groups.

This has changed a lot in recent years. After years of voting for other people, the Tea Tribes now field their own candidates, working on the remarkable fact that practically *everyone* of the right age votes. It's like they decide in one mass. Useful political tool. They also go in for some higher education.

Meanwhile, things were not going too well for the local Assamese. Remember, while these transplanted tribesmen worked on bare wages, the Brits were carving out great plantations on lands which had belonged to the Assamese. But till the 1870s or thereabouts, no local citizen was allowed to have a plantation of his own. It was only after a long time that some people made inroads.

Today there are a lot of what may be called mini-estates, but it takes a lot of land to produce tea in bulk, and a lot of bulk production to justify the humungous costs of setting up a processing plant. For e.g.: a plantation less than 12,000 hectares all around makes what is officially termed a small estate. That's still a lot of land, so there are very few individuals or families in the business.

Mostly it's companies who can have a string of estates and sustain occasional losses. Eighty-five odd kilometres east from Tezpur on the north bank of the river is Monabari, owned by Tata Tea. It is the largest functioning estate in the world. There's one bigger than it in Kenya but it's been closed for some time for some reason I can't be bothered to look up at the mo.

This here estate comes up on you sudden-like, a short distance before the Borgang river, and it is on both sides of the highway, like about 7 kilometres to a side, stretching away into the horizon.

But the real tea country, like I said, begins from Dibrugarh eastwards. Nearly 80 per cent of cultivated land in these parts is under tea, accounting for more than half of all the tea manufactured in India.

We are, you know, the world's largest tea-drinking nation. Okay, as with other figures this needs to be explained a bit. Calling us the biggest tea consumers around is a bit like sayig we have the world's second-largest civilian gun arsenal.

I see for a second there you were wondering if this was a mere arbit analogy. Well, it isn't. There are 46 million licensed firearms in India, which means more civilian guns than in any other country except the US. But the truth lies in per heads, in which case we have four guns per hundred, so don't start wearing Kevlar to office just yet. The US has 270 million firearms, which is one per person and they *should* wear Kevlar to office.

In other words, any figure in India is a huge one but has to be seen on an individual basis. We make about 800,000 tonnes of tea every year, following which we drink up 560,000 tonnes of it on our own, and while this is a lot of tea it is only about 750 grammes per year for each of us.

Most of the tea which is exported is much different from the cut-twist-curl hackjob we also call CTC, but much, much better, if made the right way and *not boiled*!!!

Assam tea as you know is distinctive and any day now it should get its Geographical Indications mark. Getting GI is like the Nobel for food products, because this means some other pretender, grown and produced elsewhere, cannot be sold under this name. Champagne, as you know, has GI, and refers only to bubbly wine from Champagne, France (Ooo, did you get conned the other day? Rofl. Reminds me of a story ... okay, some other time). So any other bubbly wine just can't be legally called champagne. I think foie gras also has a GI, not sure though.

Meanwhile, the lives of the people who produce tea are getting progressively better and perhaps they will get their full due sometime.

So, from Dibrugarh to the eastern end of the Assam Valley is a great sea of tea plantations, with bare land only an exception. Once in a while, down the road through Tinsukia to Digboi, you might find a clear meadow of rolling land and you'd say 'Ha! The Cid was wrong! This is not an estate!' But then you'll notice a big old sign facing the road which says 'Fallow Land Cleared for Planting, Owned By Klueless Bros & Co. Do Not Encroach.'

The Cid is never wrong. Get used to it. If, for the sake of argument, he is, he removes the evidence.

Say ha now, chumps.

Ed.: Ribbing the reader is a bit old hat, you know. Say ha now.

EIGHT

Digboi is the only town in India that I know means a complete sentence in English. This singular fact alone makes it worth a visit, but it has much, much more to it to justify dropping in.

It is a pure creation of the Raj, founded on the requirements or adventures of its representatives in India. Some of them left their marks in their various ways with such intensity that they left their names behind as well across the country. Macleodganj comes to mind. So does Corbett National Park, although Corbett was not only more Indian than most of his native contemporaries, but was also such an overall badass that the national park and such were the least people could do to honour his legacy.

I do not know the exact story behind Macleodganj, but perhaps someone here might tell me? Whatever the story is, I doubt it will compare with the curious case of Sleemanabad.

This little town in Madhya Pradesh is named after William Sleeman, one of the most underrated but influential British men ever to be in India. Someday someone is going to tell his story in greater detail, (John Masters already tried, in the fine 1952 novel, *The Deceivers*) but I will give a précis-like here, because, peoples, this guy was something.

Sleeman loved India from the moment he saw it: an unabashed, teenic, deep love for the land and the people which he, judging from his letters and personal thingies, did not even feel for his home island. This love was backed by a scientific mind that was part C. Auguste Dupin, part Charles Darwin.

This was about the time when central India was beset by a group of murderous bandits called the Thugs, about whom, depending on what kind of historian you've been talking to recently, you will hear different kinds of things. These guys were not only professional killers without a conscience, the type who would kick your dog just for the fun of it, but also made a name offing random travellers and merchants with *handkerchiefs and coins*. They caused as much trouble for ordinary folk as the Pindharis before them, and never mind a ridiculous movie that came out recently which allegedly shows the latter as rural freedom-fighters. Pindharis were nothing of the sort.

So, about the Thugs. Sleeman became their nemesis, getting a job as detective cum supercop of Central India in the mid-nineteenth cent, and he went after them with the full force of his will and with a systematic approach to detective work that was, remember, not very common then. He was so successful that he wiped out the Thugs virtually single-handed, among them a dude called Behram Singh, who, with an estimated 934 victims, is the most prolific recorded serial-killer ever in the world.

Well, the people of central India were so happy to see off the Thugs, this one town built a temple with Sleeman's idol in it and renamed the place in his honour. Don't believe me, you can still visit Sleemanabad and check the temple.

Oh, and before this, to prove he was even more awesome,

Sleeman went off to discover India's first-recorded dinosaur fossils in the Deccan. A proper Renaissance Man he was.

On the Sleeman mould, then, was the engineer William Lake, sharp of eye and implacable at getting things done. So this one time he was working on a new railway line for the Assam Railways and Trading Company, extending the line from Dibrugarh to Sadiya, in about 1882. Some distance from Tinsukia, he noticed a thick sludge on some of the elephants that might have been mud, but to him appeared unmudlike. What sort of guy thinks about different categories of mud, I ask? I mean, mud might have different colours and stuff but that's it, except it should be avoided where possible, is what I say.

But Lake, who either had a lot of time on his hands, or a lot of mud, smelt oil, and followed the trail to this spot where some of the sludge was oozing from the ground.

He had a working knowledge about oil extraction but, more significantly, had tonnes of enthusiasm for it, so he analysed the sample and within half a dozen years set up a small rig and poked around.

Pickings were from ground seepage in the beginning. Remember, this was a very early stage in the history of oil, with its mass commercial usage still some time in the future. It was more of a novelty to be experimented with in small doses by the pointy-heads.

By the turn of the century the Brits realised the oil reservoir went much, much deeper than they'd estimated, so they set up the Assam Oil Company in 1899.

Oil exploration was actually just that: a form of open mining. You sent a bunch of labourers to dig in the sludge, put in a hydraulic pipe and hauled the liquid out, while the scientists boiled it in a giant open vat to get various compounds, for which they scratched their heads to think up proper applications.

Lake was not content fanning himself in an armchair while the natives got to handle all that mud, so he was invariably in the pits with them through the day. The story goes that this one time, he told a labourer who was beginning to slack a bit: 'Dig, boy, dig,' which, though rude, was how the place was named.

By 1901, the Brits were salivating over just how much of the miracle crude was actually sloshing around underneath Digboi, so Asia's first and the world's second oil refinery was built. As I said, this was not the humungously complicated lights-and-clockwork systems that are called refineries today but could actually qualify as space stations. Moving on from that first open vat to a cooling and separation tower where different compounds derived from the crude were filtered and taken off, at different levels, took a long time.

With its growth and importance, the town boomed with workers and technicians arriving from everywhere, and it became the first of Assam's several oil and coal townships.

The oil reserves here ran out in 1934, but by then about a thousand wells had been dug up. This place was where some of the pioneers in deep oil exploration learnt their ropes. Exploration at other places nearby and in northern Burma continued, from where the crude was piped here in a steady flow, so today Digboi is the world's oldest functioning refinery. Today, with no more crude from Myanmar following Independence, and the Numaligarh refinery in Golaghat the new kid on the block, the inflow from oilfields at Ledo, Namrup and other towns in Upper Assam is considerably less, but like I imagine Lake must have been, Digboi is going gamely with the flow and abides.

I have many wonderful memories of growing up in this place. Most of my summer and winter vacations were spent here with my grandparents, and at a time when Guwahati was a somewhat haphazard and occasionally chaotic place, the customary system and civic order in Digboi was like another world.

Like most industrial towns, Digboi's population is constant, which fact itself makes handling things like housing and urban infrastructure less of a headache than elsewhere. The roads have always been teutonically smooth and clean, the houses neat, shops and such in reasonable order, and there were even neat chocolate-block footpaths back when Guwahati's city sport was first being discovered and perfected.

Back in the day, if you were from Digboi you said it with a great measure of pride, because it was leading the pack in the oil business, Assam's third-biggest industry after tea and timber. Eventually, the people of Digboi became so thoroughly Britified that they have since held on to all the lifestyle and entertainment thingies of that period and kept at it.

Which is why an evening at its old officers' clubs or its tennis courts is among the best ways to spend a leisurely vacation, if you get accommodation at one of the lodges. If you can further manage to play a few rounds as guest at the golf course, which is hands down one of the finest in the whole of eastern India, man, you got it made.

The roads out of Digboi are the only grouse I have with industrial towns in Upper Assam, because all of them, without exception, are crappy, like they make up for all that order and system by having bad roads so other people will stay away, or perhaps the PWD takes revenge on these companies out of spite.

A little distance away is the Lakhipathar Reserved Forest, which till a while ago was an excellent place if you were the hunting kind, with a lot of wild pig and swamp fowl, both of which are very difficult to bring back for lunch.

This recreational hunting was another casualty of insurgency. In 1990, the Army, on the first of their two major operations against the ULFA, found huge mass graves where militants had dumped their victims, and Lakhipathar's name was forever blackened. Even today, people do not pass through the denser parts of the place without a shudder.

All this makes Digboi an excellent staging point to look at both the tea and oil industries of Upper Assam. Moreover, once you are there, you must absolutely visit the Oil Museum which is the only one of its kind in India, dunno if there are any as marvellous in the world. I seriously doubt there is something as extensive or passionately constructed in, say, Riyadh.

For in this oil museum, over an entire first floor of man-sized panels with text, illustrations, maps and photographs, you can read about the story of oil, not just in Upper Assam, but how, over time, the fuel got to where it is today, one of the single-most potent factors in world politics. You get to see blurred pictures of pioneers like Lake and the appropriately-named Goodenough, another drill-maniac, how they lived in the dense forests with their backs to the wild, chasing what was an entirely new frontier. You see the old machines and rigs used back then, a highly-detailed model of the refinery as it exists today, you get to see objects and instruments of office and personal use spanning over a hundred years, you see vehicles which might be rare even for an antique car rally, a real first-generation petrol pump complete in every detail (which might even pump oil but I've never tried it, maybe will sometime).

The museum complex is built around the first oil well and a profound site it is, this simple rig about 50 feet high. The staff at the museum will be happy to show you around, although taking photographs is not allowed, tempting though the idea is.

The Cid, riding on pure awesomeness and characteristic name-dropping, does get his pics but what'd you think of me if I didn't document this place? Dude, in this remote (I do not like using this word because it tends to get misused more often than not, but Digboi is indeed far down the eastern narrow road, so this time) and peaceful little town where cars once used to compete to allow the other the right of passage, a place filled with chronically nice people to its gills, this place is the unlikeliest spot you can imagine where you can sit and think about the history of the industry most directly responsible for pollution, wars and strife for much of the last three decades.

Inside the museum complex is also what is, I believe, the last functional bunker-cum-air raid shelter of the Second World War in this part of the world. Back then, the Japanese cunningly bombed the Burma-Assam crude pipeline that fed to this town, and you can see some of the damaged pipes as well, just as they used to be. Digboi was a high-value target for Japanese bombers, so this bunker was among several which came up. This one is in reasonably good shape, while you can find several more in northern Myanmar, but those are risky to enter. This one is about six feet deep, smells a little mouldy but is maintained well by the museum people.

A little southeast from Digboi, along another bone-rearranging set of roads is Ledo, another town floating on oil, near the Myanmar border and leading to the Pangsau Pass from were it is a direct line through a densely-forested valley into northern Myanmar. Ledo used to be the starting point of the famous Stilwell Road. The road was built to parallel the India-Burma oil pipeline during the war and eventually ended at Kunming in China. Its main purpose, as the name taken from the commander of the American army on this front suggests, was to supply Chinese fighters against the Japanese. After the war, its purpose over and with two countries coming up in place of the old empire, and with communist China erasing the history of Allied help without a second thought, the Stilwell Road closed down and was eaten by the ever-present jungle.

For a few years there has been a lot of talk about India's Look East Policy, which says the North-east's massive border with Myanmar and China should be open for trade and things, based on the typical South Block premise that transport being a big problem from the rest of the country to the region, people here might as well trade with neighbouring countries which have relatively easier access. This doctrine, thought not without possibilities, overlooks some basic ground realities which seem trivial at the mo but which will rear up and bite South Block in sensitive parts if given half the chance.

My editor in Guwahati back then had explained that trade between the North-east and neighbouring countries could only be a just relationship if the region was producing goods of sufficient volume and quality to trade on an equal basis with them. There is, after all, no point if trade means us buying Chinese goods all the time, is it, and I do not see what we can offer them in equivalent bulk as things stand today.

The other little thing is, see, trade never stopped entirely in these parts. It is just that this trade is mostly in firearms and drugs, and a more open border will mean more of these, and more corrupt border forces and what not. Big problems, man, so these need to be solved before we hove out the garlands for our beloved neighbours.

Anyhow, the Stilwell Road is being repaired as we speak, as part of this lame-brained doctrine, and will eventually reach the old last stop at Kunming. Regardless of the politico-economic fallout, this will be one road trip totally worth going on, because no one has been on it in the past sixty-five years and, woo, there will be so much new to see, so the Cid is waiting.

Along this border are a few open points where neighbouring villages and towns trade across the international line, same as Moreh in southern Manipur where we will eventually reach on this trip. Eighty-odd kilometres from Digboi is also the infamous Lake of No Return, and you should see that place.

Today the lake is a cute little place with a village next to it, a restful spot with all kinds of birds chirping in the trees, where you can sit underneath a tree, ignore the warnings by locals who might tell you to watch out for elephants in the evening, and generally let time pass you by.

Back during the war, though, this was a mystery to rival the Bermuda Triangle. This one time in 1943 or thereabouts, Allied soldiers stationed near the lake started disappearing in numbers alarming to the command. Theories began to abound. Japanese spies and special forces, said some. Others said in an area this densely forested, there was no telling if some ancient monster, fundamentally opposed for some lame reason to men in uniform, had started preying on soldiers. Yet others claimed there was some kind of light within the lake or Shyamalanesque mist which took away men, never to be found.

About a couple years into these vanishings the soldiers eventually solved the mystery. Some nutcase locals had been offing the men on a crazy idea of hawking their valuables and making a buck or two. Must have thought these strange big white men were more loaded than they looked. Like I said, nuts.

But the name stuck, so if you happen to pass by the Lake of No Return today, you might stop awhile. Around this corner of Upper Assam are also other industrial towns, because this place is not just floating on oil, but also natural gas, such as at Namrup, or coal, which is everywhere. It is the economic backbone of Assam. Further east begins one of the most interesting states in this all-round interesting corner of the world.

NINE

Arunachal Pradesh is a special land. The thing that makes it even more special than expected for me is, however, a small bit of demographics.

Ordinarily, I don't go much by statistics, particularly any figures about India. I find most such numbers obsolete, suspiciously round-figured or, erm, confusing. I take a look at the, say, *Index of Multi-Racial Transmogrification in the Upper Nilgiris with Respect to Secondary Sectoral Productivity* and I am taken aback. The numbers, frequently in the millions, of whichever unit is the flavour of the day, jump out and hit me betwixt the eyes, as it were. So I see a bunch of numbers coming, I walk the opposite way. Never trusted them to either inform or entertain me.

Demographics, that one sub-stratum amid this humungous numberdom, is a major problem. I mean, seriously. You run your eyes down a column of population data or census report and you get to *feel* the rush of more than a billion feet. The magnitude of even apparently trivial indexes of human activity in this country is immense. And yet they base most figures on per capita. Strange.

Well, we are due for another census next year, but meanwhile, do take a look at a small column called population density, will you? Delhi, where I live these days, has (on *sarkari* paper) 9,294 people per sq. km. I think about this figure sometimes. This means every time I am out on the street, taking a square with each side of length

1 km, there are 9,293 other poor souls in this same blessed square as me. It is a tidal wave, my friends, a freaking tidal wave of humanity, that's what it is, yes. (This average, according to highly misplaced unofficial sources, is significantly higher inside government-operated liquor stores on the eve of a national holiday or festival or some such.)

Alright, so round about now you will have looked down the left column of this table and are prolly saying Delhi is on this list because it is a Union Territory. Excellent point. Take just the states then.

West Bengal is the super-champ here. We find 900-odd people per sq. km in that state, and considering how relatively small it is, it must be kind of crowded there too. The usual suspects, UP and Bihar (what would we do without them, eh?) try their best to be in the game, scoring a bit above 689 and 880 respectively or thereabouts. Kerala does very well in this too, I've been told.

And at this point we ask: where, then, are there fewer people to be found? Naturally, the hill-states. But before that, do remember that 1 sq. km is a very small area by itself, so if you are a visual kind of person and picturing a square of that dimension and putting people inside them, chances are the box is more crowded than you imagine.

So, Kashmir has 99 people per sq. km, not counting, I suppose, the odd terrorists or security fellows lurking in the bushes and chasing one another. These, owing to their methods of operation, might be constantly on the move and might be leaving the box shortly, and I hope you don't meet them. But if even 99 people in a box that size is too crowded for you, keep looking.

Here it comes, at last: on any given day in Arunachal,

you will find 11 people in a sq. km area. So if you take a cricket team into Arunachal, there will be legitimate reasons for accusing you of upsetting the demographics of that blessed place. But, generally, there it is: the least populated state in India and therefore even more awesome than it is.

On any given day in Arunachal, if you were to take a walk (which I hope you do, because I like walkers) you would meet maybe two or three people in the area herebefore mentioned. The rest, on careful inquiry, you will discover are either a. at home and minding their own business; b. cooking some exotic food thingy that they'll be damned before sharing with a nosey tourist or c. gathered with their pals and getting drunk and thanking the good Donyi-Polo or Buddha up in the sky for sparing them the questions of people who should have stayed at home with *their* friends to begin with.

The walker in Arunachal thus gets the feeling of being left to his own devices, which, as I have discovered, adds to a feeling of general happiness and joy with the state of things and with the world. The weather is excellent, the wind is blowing down from the north and has a bit of reassuring bite to it, the piney hills are engaged in a friendly debate with the deciduous about which variety should take precedence, there is a lot of white on the horizon which are snowy mountains which you should be trying to climb instead of gawking at them from inside a Tata Sumo and taking pics, and, look closely under that shrub: that's prolly a bug you've never seen before and neither has science. And there is a familiar scent in the air that you're sure you can identify without digging out a local to do your legwork for you. Can you, now?

Orchids, man. Orchids.

Aside from being *the* most structurally interesting flower around (how else am I to estimate a flower, huh? You don't want me to actually smell it, do you?), orchids are also demanding little critters. They need the right altitude, right climate, not too much heat or dry air, a sort of moist lab condition. Being picky about how they choose to live, orchids take a lot of persuasion to diversify. India has about 900 orchid species. Six hundred-odd are native to Arunachal.

The valleys of Arunachal, just below those snowy mountains that you see, get what weather people call 'a humid climate of the sub-tropical variety, sir', which basically means summers are hot and damp and you perspire, and beer is a good option, and winters are kind of cool. And— bingo!—the state gets about 4,000 mm of rainfall every year, year on year, which is, I am told, equivalent to like 20 million tin buckets of good clear water splashing all over the place. All this creates pockets within these valleys which become like giant hothouses where various kinds of vegetation grow. Among them are dozens of varieties of orchids including some which are virtually impossible to transplant and grow elsewhere (trust me, some scientist types keep going down to these valleys and carting away flowers to grow them elsewhere).

The upshot of all this vegetation picnic is Arunachal is a treasure-house of incredible biodiversity (finally a word whose meaning I know. I like using such words: they make me sound real smart).

Meanwhile, the slopes of the mountains are no less diversely vegetated, with vast stretches of teak and sal, oak, fir, pine and even maple, covering, I'm told, more than 60,000 sq. km, and I am not even kidding. Maybe even more because the forests look very big.

The major people of Arunachal are the Nishi, Adi and Monpa. If you remember (which you should) over 50 dialects are spoken here, but Assamese is like a link language.

Take a map of Arunachal, and draw a line from its western to its eastern border, bisecting it roughly in half. This will help understanding its history and possibly some of China's delusions, on which I shall discourse at length because it is a b-i-i-g grouse I have with that there country.

This line could be said to be how Arunachal has been for most of the last millennium. South of this line, which, ye smart people, would include the foothills, the land was under the Ahom kings. North of this line, as evidenced today by the predominance of Buddhism, the people settled here were from Tibet or were of Tibetan stock. Umm, I guess that would mean the same thing, wouldn't it? Wait a sec, wait a sec. This anthropology business can get confusing. Yes, I think that's about correct. Let's just say north of our line there were people of Tibetan stock who, at some point in history, must have trundled in from Tibet, seeing as Tibetans come from Tibet and not, say, Hissar.

So we have Tibetans in the north, various tribes in the south governed by Ahoms in Assam, and some tribes spread across the line who wouldn't give two hoots for boundaries and as soon as whack you upside the head as look at you if you went to explain it to them.

You got to understand something about the way places

were administered back then, particularly places as inaccessible as most of the North-east. No vehicles, mostly no roads and telecom, so administration was not exactly hands-on. Sometime over the early part of the last millennia, during the summers, a draggled bunch of officials in their robes would come fluttering through some pass from Lhasa into northern Arunachal, take a look around to see if everything was well and maybe collect the taxes if they were up to it. The *idea* that a piece of territory was under them was more important than the actual enforcement of that idea, which seems a very sensible notion to me, and much better than marching semi-clad monk armies through sub-zero mountain passes with the windchill taking off tiny parts of men and animals.

Say I'm a Buddhist monk deputed by the big guys in Lhasa. 'You, there,' they say (I'm assuming I'm too lowly for them to remember my name). 'You, there. Be a nice fellow and pop down to Upper Arunachal (or whatever they called it, I'm too lazy to look it up) and see if the lamas are saying their prayers and if the people acknowledge us, will you? Return in a decade or so, if you feel like it.' And me, I would do the popping down, and possibly not return because life is too short to go running up and down dadgum mountains when I could spend my time smelling the orchids, right? Life went on. That, I am told, is just how places like Tawang were connected with Tibet. Hardly what one would call jurisdiction or national boundary, would one?

Afterwards, the Brits came and made a deal with Tibet and fixed the boundary as it is shown on Indian maps today, and Tibet agreed, so where does China come in?

Nowhere, that's where. In the first place, its occupation of Tibet is illegal and cruel, and its demands on Arunachal idiotic at best.

Btw, Arunachal was called NEFA by the Brits, short for North East Frontier Agency, a compass-counterpart to the North West Frontier Province in our beloved neighbour, and such a contrast these two places are.

The NWFP, when the British managed to set up some kind of administration there, was always a restive place, home to warring tribes who never got (and still don't get) concepts that we take for granted, like urban development, taxes, elected authority, respect for the law or even some things called 'state' and 'government'. Barely a day went by back then when the British Indian Army didn't have to saddle up and go after insurgents, rebels, village chieftains on the run, brigands and such.

NEFA did not make a peep, and Arunachal is one of the most peaceful states in the country even today. Religion, I believe, has a lot to do with it, as does the temperament of the people. Buddhist monasteries dot the northern part of Arunachal, the most famous and powerful being Tawang. Built in the seventeenth century, Tawang is a big name for Buddhists everywhere.

Back then, the Fifth Dalai Lama himself asked one of his trusted followers to visit the area and build a big monastery. So the dude set off, but on arriving seems to have had some problems deciding on an exact spot for the complex. At this point his horse seems to have decided it for him by vanishing. The beast was found a day or so afterwards standing at a spot, so the monk, happy to have some sign from the heavens to make up his mind for him, started building the monastery on that hilltop. That's why the place was called *Ta Wang*, which means 'Selected By The Horse', although it is unfair that we do not know the horse's name today (or maybe someone does and I haven't asked yet).

Tawang grew in size and reputation and hosted hundreds of learned monks from here and Tibet and always had close links with Lhasa, of the spiritual kind, I must add. The original building was cracking in places so in 1997 it was rebuilt in concrete. It is three storeys high and has this simply marvellous library with all kinds of historically and religiously important documents and scrolls that some of you might find useful to go through. There are a few guys there who can show you around and supervise while you examine the scrolls, and they'll be happy to guide you.

You can also drop in and meet monks in their residential quarters where, apart from the close smell of incense which some people find a bit thick indoors, you get to learn a lot about the place and about neighbouring people too, such as the Monpas, who have been part of the local Buddhist backbone. Fascinating place, excellent weather most of the year, altitude a little above 3,300 metres, simply divine sunrises, particularly in autumn.

North and west of Tawang you can go on for about 20 km before the army turns you back because beyond that is restricted.

To reach the monastery, you take the Saraighat Bridge north from Guwahati and then go east through Mangaldoi on the north bank to Tezpur, another ancient town (think I mentioned it somewhere earlier). From Tezpur you go north over the plains till you reach the hills and then proceed north-west to Bomdila, about six hours by road in good weather. Tawang is an equal distance from Bomdila.

Which reminds me: there's a bit of paperwork involved with travelling in the North-east that you need to get sorted out, depending on whether you are from India or abroad. This comes from it being a border region and because most parts are difficult to access so the government needs to make sure there is a proper record of who's going where.

If you are an Indian, you need to get what is called an Inner Line Permit, for Arunachal, Nagaland and Mizoram. You can get these permits from the political secretaries of the state governments; it's a fairly easy process and not a hassle. You've got to make sure you carry these permits safely while on the road, and show them at checkposts at the borders. Thassall. There is otherwise no restriction on how many are travelling in your group, or how you are travelling, so long as you have the paper, and you don't need this for the other states.

If, on the other hand, you are a *firang* . . . hang on a sec, please. If you *are* a *firang*, don't mind us calling you that because it comes from this Persian word, you see, which in turn was derived from 'Frank', the name of the people who led the Crusades back in the day. Since the Franks were originally Vikings, you should not mind the name. *I* wouldn't mind being called a Viking.

Ed.: In another age, your digressions would have been called 'scholarly', I suppose.

Erm. So, if you are a *firang*, you need to get a Protected Area Permit. This permit, incid., is also needed if you are to travel in some parts of J&K, Himachal and, I think, Uttarakhand. In the North-east, you need it for four states: Arunachal, Manipur, Mizoram and Nagaland. You can get this document at Indian embassies everywhere, or from the ministry of home affairs, or the political secretaries of these states. A permit is usually issued for ten days, but you can extend it by another week. Since you might have to do a deal of waiting to get the extension, I'd say make up your mind first so you won't need to apply in the middle of your trip or something. If you are from Pakistan, Myanmar, Bangladesh or China, however, you can get the permit only from the ministry of home affairs.

Unlike the Inner Line Permit, the Protected Area Permit comes with some riders you got to keep in mind. You can't, sadly, travel alone. You'll need to be in a group of at least four people, accompanied by a travel agent, and you have to make sure that guy is registered with whichever agency is in charge of registering him.

There are also some parts where, despite the permit, you will not be allowed to enter, so bear that in mind. Bet the document will explain about these parts. There are also specific points through which you are to enter or leave.

For Indians, though, the Inner Line Permit is a breeze, so don't let *that* stop you from making a plan. After all, you take the trouble for a Restricted Area Permit for the Andamans, don't you, so the paperwork should not be an excuse.

Me? I don't need a permit for the North-east. The only document I have is my own awesomeness.

Alright: Indian journalists don't need permits. Happy? You wanted me to admit that bit, didn't you?

While on Tawang, you can guess how important the monastery is if I tell you that one of the Dalai Lamas, prolly the sixth if I remember correctly, was born here. It is a beautiful and peaceful place where you should go before the diabolical and fiendish Potato-Chips Tourists swarm in and ruin everything. Oh ho ho, wait, I've got this thing I've got to tell you first.

Y'see, I've got a name for these tourists. I call them Joeys. How it came about is, thusly: I was once at Guwahati airport, in line with a bunch of other poor suckers at security check, where these days you unload your electronic thingies into trays and shuffle along under beepers and scanners. So we were standing there to be duly processed, and then I was first in line, just about to go in, when the CISF fellow waves at me to stop, and motions to his side. I look, and behold, I see this fat man, his wife and two dumb-looking young men, perhaps in their early twenties. F.m. is obviously some kind of bureaucrat, high-ranking too, by the looks of him, and his wife, guess what she was holding in her hand, peoples? Yes, that's right, a pack of potato chips, I swear. A pack of potato chips when they are about to go into a supposedly high-security zone where you are certainly not allowed to go munching around the place. They'd been touristing in the region and were heading back, it appeared, and of course they wouldn't stand in line, would they? So they waltzed right in, and there wasn't no security check either. I was returning to Delhi after a longish trip and too tired to give my 'Long Live the Proletariat' speech, but those faces, they're seared into my memory. I remember you, dude. I remember your whole family. I also remember I'd been in line for more than an hour that day, man.

And, ma'am, I remember that you turned around and yelled to the younger son: 'Come along, Joey.' So the name. See, I made you famous. If you read this and want to throw down, contact me. I never forget.

I sometimes wonder about Joey. What sort of a person is he, I ask, to be compelled to tag along with a father who looks like he became a civil servant because he sucked at everything else. (Oh, wait, most c.s-es *are* like that, so I take back my words.) Joey himself looked like Arm Fall Off Boy, and while looking like a superhero might be considered an advantage in some circles, would anyone live a life looking like Arm Fall Off Boy without suffering intense psych trauma?

(Note: A.F.O. Boy is a little-known superhero from the 1980s. His superpower was he could detach his left arm and beat people with it. Serious. The Legion of Superheroes rejected him at an audition. Man, I'm not making this up.)

So we can sympathise a little with Joey because of his appearance and parentage, but not much. If we were to look further into his life, what would emerge? A young man who texts 'Sry wnt cme 2 prty sme wrk cme up b4 cld rch lol, vil b dere tmrw, c u' on a *full-text* keypad. I mean, there is such a thing as a dictionary in a cellphone, but Joey will not use it, will he, not even when the correct spelling takes the same number of keystrokes as his lobotomised message. But then, Joey won't spell things right on his comp either and what does LOL mean here anyway? Does he mean he is laughing out loud while saying sorry he won't be at the 'prty'? Why not use emoticons, idiot, when *that's what they're for?*

Perhaps he can actually differentiate between different

brands of hair gel and other such lame stuff, pretends to like electronica when electronica went out last week and says things like 'presently' when he means 'currently' and doesn't stop at traffic signals because his daddy told him the little blinky lights are for other people, so he is beyond the pale.

Ed.: Getting a bit hyper, are we?

So, yeah, coming back to Tawang, do make it quick before the Joeys of the world mess it up and the lamas shut the big doors of the venerable monastery right on your face.

Apart from Buddha, the other big guy in these parts is Donyi-Polo, deity of a religion whose exact beliefs and tenets, I trust, you will find out on your own because I don't know enough to tell you. Suffice it that I have brought it to your notice and it is a cool name for a god.

All kinds of tribes here, as usual, with the Monpas dominating in the east. In the centre of the state are Nishi and Apatani, in the east, Adi, Minyong and many, many more. In easternmost Arunachal are the two districts of Tirap and Changlang, where you'd find large concentrations of Nagas. Some of these tribes are animists, and have remained so despite Buddha, Christ and some Hindu gods trudging by now and then. That's something. Other tribes have shamans. Yes—actual, home-grown shamans, some with masks and spirit communication and the whole shebang. I need to look into this in more detail one of these days, although it must be said that genuine shamans, and tribes which practise shamanism, have retreated further into the wilds and are cautious about visitors, having burnt their fingers with some *firang* anthropologist types who, I heard, occasionally whacked major artifacts.

Shamanism revolves around the power of artifacts to a large extent, so one can imagine the damage this must have done. Poor shaman wakes up one morning and goes into his spirit-calling hut to have a morning editorial session with his guiding spirits to settle the agenda of the harvest season, and yipe! the sacred spirit-calling mask, a never-failing hotline to the big guys, is gone. So you will have to search a lot, not only for people who practise these rituals the old way, but who also believe in them. *That* is more difficult to find in these benighted times.

Hinduism, someone asked? It seems, since most of the foothills have been accessible through history, Hinduism made some inroads once in a while. In the West Siang district lies the Siang hill range. At the base of these hills, some ruins have been discovered, Inca-style, of stone-built Hindu temples, mainly of Mother Goddess worship, which used to be big in neighbouring parts of Assam. These ruins are from the Malini Than complex of temples, of which the oldest are about six hundred years old and maybe even older. But that appears to be the deepest Hinduism could penetrate.

I think I mentioned a while back that 1962 was when the people of Assam first began having serious doubts about their place in India. It was with the way events unfolded, and how the Centre reacted to it. There are many things this country needs to learn from that episode.

The war with China is a part of Independent India's history which is, curiously, not talked about much. Okay, we lost (yes we did, you know) so maybe that is a very good reason not to talk about it, but some analysis once in a while would have been proper, don't you think? The only time I read of the war is when China makes demands on Arunachal. People don't even remark anymore on the fact that this big slice of Ladakh is included in China in maps printed abroad. And here back in school we used to draw maps of the country as it was, for like a week or so before PoK was cut out.

But the China war affected a big part of the country so it should be discussed sometimes. In autumn 1962, with the world occupied with the Cuban Missile Crisis between the two superpowers back then, China saw its chance and sent troops into Ladakh and Arunachal.

They say India made the first moves, shifting border fences here and there. I dunno which is which. See, *that's* why we need to talk about it.

The point is, about 80,000 Chinese troops entered these two areas. Against them, at maximum deployment during the war, were about 12,000 Indian soldiers, a fact you will remark on immediately. Anyway there was some hard fighting at altitudes where a brisk walk will leave you gasping for breath and shivering in the harsh light of a summer's day, so you can imagine the difficulties the men faced.

You know, Indian soldiers fought in tennis shoes with bolt-action rifles against what were new AK-56s and properly-clothed Chinese. It was a half-hearted fight, is what it was. All that combined into retreat after retreat for India, till China had Aksai Chin and had reached Tezpur in Assam.

Civilians who were already fleeing from this invasion saw the troops come in to defend their lands. They could count, you know. That's how they realised the troops were far fewer than what they should have been. So they asked one another: where was the Indian Army, the fourth (or is it fifth) largest standing army in the world? Just what was going on?

And the defence minister back then, or somebody, advised against air strikes for no apparent reason. And then Nehru made the one statement which people in Assam were to remember afterwards. He said: 'My heart goes out to the people of Assam.'

It was absolutely the wrong thing to say. Perhaps he meant it well; certainly he was an erudite man and could come up with learned expressions. But how do you explain that to a people who expected him to respond with troops, and not just sympathy?

In that winter, with soldiers on both sides freezing to death on their feet, the Chinese retreated. They kept Aksai Chin, though, and the highest ridges along the Arunachal border. The people in the mountains went back home, and so did the people in Assam, but over the years India increased its military presence in Arunachal, so you will keep coming across military checkpoints on the roads here, and some areas are off-limits, scenic though they are.

That was the war no one talks about, and that invasion turned Arunachal into a perpetual frontline zone and the people of Assam to decidedly secessionist thoughts, for some time.

Travel in Arunachal is illustrative of the peculiar transport problems in the North-east. Sometimes, to travel from one part of the state to the other, you have to come down to the plains because there is simply no direct route. For instance, what if you wanted to travel from Tawang, at the western tip, to Itanagar, state capital, far to the east? You come down, through Bomdila to Tezpur and then go east over the Brahmaputra valley, finally climbing into the hills again to reach Itanagar. Or if you want to go to east Arunachal from just a few kilometres away in Dibrugarh. Either you chance the mountain roads which might or might not be open, or you go to the bridge at Tezpur, return east along the north bank another two hundred kilometres, and then hit the hills. These are matters which sound funny when narrated but which have been a fact of life for people here. They just shrug and chug along, but things could have been so much better.

The fast streams and rivers that flow down through Arunachal, which make road travel a hassle in the absence of concrete bridges, however, make up a bit with some great fishing spots, particularly in September and October, just before winter sets in and the *mahseer* are fattest.

Arunachal, for the traveller, is *that* close to being perfect. So some jackass had to spoil it. Suddenly, as it were, there were prospectors and lame scientist-types swarming over the mountains and before you went there twice there were 42 power projects signed and ready, and big trucks and excavators mucking around all over digging and looking important. These dams and hydro-electric plans might bring power to the rest of the region, and power is something the region needs a lot, but these dams are like everywhere, it seems. Not one place in the lower mountains that you knew of can you visit today without being jumped on by random crewmen or getting tangled in barbed-wire with 'Keep Out' notices and such. They could have begun a few projects at a time, but that would be sensible and it is not done that way, is it?

Some of these super-mega dams have displaced entire ancient settlements and also threaten some extremely finely-balanced eco-systems. I am neither for nor against dams. If they benefit people and bring electricity to the energy-starved North-east and create some employment, fine. But most of the contractors are not from around there, so you only guess at who benefits from all that money pouring in and scams all over the place. Yep, the same contractors and interests who benefit from other projects elsewhere.

You have to travel in Arunachal a deal to discover for yourself how beautiful and precious a natural heritage it is, and why it should be preserved not just as an example of what the earth once was, but also in the best interests of science.

I have, incredibly, sounded very wise in the last para. It took a lot of effort.

TEN

From Digboi I return west through, counting from right to left on the map, Dibrugarh, Sivasagar and Jorhat to Golaghat, from where I head by night bus south to Dimapur. It rains during the journey, as it has since I left Guwahati. Either a drizzle or a proper downpour, but it rains in a constant torrent the entire time I'm on the bus. This, says the Cid to himself, might be a bother if the main body of the monsoon is here already, because it will bring twenty kinds of problems in the hills, the biggest being blocked roads.

The route the bus takes is along the rise of the Karbi Anglong hills on the west. This, as I've mentioned somewhere, is a hill district and one of the parts of Assam which was in tribute-paying relations with the kingdom. So the Karbis were among the earliest to begin demanding some kind of autonomy or a state, after which they got an autonomous district.

Despite this, Karbi Anglong has never really been at peace because of a bunch of different-coloured militant groups, some of which are so small it is comical. I mean, they could actually be like five men with a stick for all they're worth, because they've got into the militancy business and, with other groups of little relevance and minor nuisance value, turned insurgency into a cottage industry. You make a group, attack someone as a way to let everyone else know there's a new group on the block, and then get to the really relevant part of the deal: designing a symbol. This you get printed on a sheaf of A4 paper, write an extortion note in bad grammar and awful handwriting and send it to whoever you think has enough money to pay up. Thus you have a good business running in a place you'll never find a good job and if there was a good job it would go to someone better suited to it, so you will extort from him instead.

I should add here that this kind of cottage industry had its golden age a while ago and things are becoming saner by the day.

However, remember that Karbi Anglong and other parts of the North-east have a glorious tangle of ethnic movements and settlements in their past, so equations are always complicated. These equations, no matter what the future of insurgency, will not go away quickly, and as populations grow and old divides deepen with economic pressures and such, ethnic strife becomes more common. A while ago there was deal of fighting between the majority Karbis and the Kukis who live here. Sometime after that the Karbis must have gone on a substance-abuse spree because they attacked the Jaintias of eastern Meghalaya, some of whom live in the next-door hills of KA. It is a very messy business and something or the other keeps going belly-up in Karbi Anglong. Until matters get sorted out, this hill district is a place best left alone.

The road on which my bus is lurching down south next to the Karbi Hills is not smooth and was, perhaps, never meant to be. It is an established rule of the universe almost. They will pave over the whole of the earth and build sky elevators, and yet, when some guest comes visiting down the Golaghat-Dimapur road it will still jar his backbone. In fact, in a great feat of collective self-negation or some other word which might be more appropriate here but which I cannot remember, the locals have stopped asking that the road be fixed and possibly are not sure who is in charge of it in the first place. It could be the Assam PWD ministry. So it won't be fixed; so stop complaining.

This stretch is also somewhat thinly populated and heavily forested, so you will not see much outside your window on a dark night except maybe a few settlements here and there. It is the idiomatic backyard of the Assam Valley, this thin stretch of plainland between the Karbi and Naga Hills. There is, however, a significant number of migrant settlers so this could be a potential flashpoint in the future.

By the time I reach Dimapur early the next morning, the rain, which has not let up at all, has become a heavy shower, which adds to the backache this road inevitably builds up. Dimapur is the gateway to the Naga Hills and beyond, and is in the plains. It was the capital of the Dimasa kingdom back before the Ahoms captured it. Since then, it has functioned as a trading post between the plains and the hills and today is a major trade centre, transport hub and the keystone to Nagaland's economy, being the last real plainstown before it is hills all the way to the southern tip of Mizoram. Everything that sustains three states and millions of people passes through Dimapur, since the other route through Silchar, south of Karbi Anglong, is very sticky these days.

Dimapur, therefore, suffers from a glut of truck repair workshops and all manner of grubby eating places and decrepit establishments and migrants. It is also usually dusty and has rashes of garbage everywhere, which means it is not a pretty sight during the rains.

It might be in Nagaland alright, but the Nagas are never sure about who runs the private sector in this town. Control over the truck, bus, clothing and other businesses which feed into the hills has swung back and forth between various groups. Back in the days when Naga insurgency was still on, much of this control was in local hands. Today, thirteen years into peace, migrant-owned businesses are on the rise. This has led to friction and if someday there is strife between the Nagas and migrants, it will be because of this. By migrants I refer here to illegally resident Bangladeshis.

You won't find many of them in the hills of the region, though there are several settlements today along the southern foothills of Meghalaya. They mostly prefer the easy pickings and softer life in the Brahmaputra Valley, as I said. Dimapur is sort of their last outpost, and you bet they keep trying to take it over. But the Nagas are not only a doughty bunch, they know business as well as anyone else, I assure you, so it will not be such an easy job for Bangladeshis here. But, yes, there are far too many migrant labourers, mechanics and such here to make it a comfortable staging post.

Dimapur's city sport is the Great Crappy Restaurant Food Game which, if you reach by night bus as is usual, you might have to participate in. Connecting transport from the bus depot leave frequently for Kohima, so you will only have sufficient time for a bite at one of half a million eateries in the neighbourhood. Speaking of eateries,

You can almost *see* the waves of badass anger from Lachit's face. Generalling in those days wasn't easy, even for a military genius and a patriot.

They sure went on and on carting up oil, beginning from this one, Digboi's first oil well. Lake practically dug this on his own, you know.

'When you go home, tell them of us and say/ For your tomorrow, we gave our today.' Heard that before? It comes from the inscription on this here cemetery wall.

From April to June 1944, this hillside, where the cemetery is today, saw some of the bitterest fighting in the Burma Campaign. This is holy ground, man.

Basic info about the men who died in the Campaign is on their graves, including regiment, age and religion…

… but don't look to their religious symbols for their stories. Those were incidental.

We don't know his age or his homeland or his religion. I can't even pronounce his name. But he was one hell of a man. They all were.

Rudyard Kipling composed this phrase in memory of his son, whose body was never identified.

During the worst of the fighting, the men shot at each other across this tennis court, where the cross stands today. At night, they could hear their enemies breathing.

And then the Kohima mist sneaks up and blots out the world. Awesomeness.

The Kohima Catholic Cathedral is a mecha-gigantor homage to the war dead by Japanese visitors and locals.

SENAPATI DISTRICT STUDENTS' ASSOCIATION (SDSA)

Senapati District H.Q.

Ref. No. ....

Date 08/05/08

PERM IT CARD

TO WHOM IT MAY CONCERN

Kindly allow the bearer of this Permit Card to pass through .... Senapati to Imphal .... *The Vehicle bearing registration No. :* AS01F 0544 *is permitted after necessary verification by the concern authorities.*

Thanking you.

Date: 08/05/08

Yours sincerely

(KUEA PETER)
President, SDSA.
President
Senapati District Students' Assn.

Told you I had a pic of the dashed permit Manipuri student groups issue to truckers in Senapati district. This is scamland.

One of the palace/temple/ pavilions inside Kangla Fort, from where the bosses then used to watch plays and such at the amphitheatre behind me.

Three fat dragons standing in a row, and I don't know if one is extra or the Brits were playing a trick in their pics.

Impressive even today, but the new(er) gate at Kangla Fort is a dadgum pale copy of the original, imho.

That sepak takraw ball there in mid-air among a Meitei and three Tamils. Can't believe I got an unblurred image of the ball. *Merci*, cam.

In the early afternoon, from the nearest point I can click the border, with people hauling their stuff across. Time to cross, homies.

I do not much like using that word but I have run out of synonyms for 'restaurant' and '*dhaba*' would be an inappropriate description of these joints, so we'll continue.

In these Dimapur restaurants, then, which have uniformly rude or squint-eyed waiters and minimal hygiene, the menu, at first glance, appears to be a delight. You smile a satisfied smile when you read 'Mutton', 'Beef' and 'Pork' (but, alas, seldom 'Fish'). You say to yourself: Ha, now we are talking. Here is where we stock up for the uphill stage. You will, however, be mistaken.

For the thing that comes floating on a lagoon of oil of dubious nature cannot be strictly categorised in any regular meat grouping. What is it? you wonder. Is it, perhaps, mutton? But it does not have the regular chewiness or salty flavour of good goatmeat. Is it beef, then? Perhaps. It is definitely not pork, and if it is, where is the two-inch-thick trim of fat that by legal definition should accompany each piece? Did the cook whack it? Is this a new and yet-unheard-of level of health-freakhood: meat from an actual low-fat pig taught from childhood to do weird aerobics?

Such vital existential questions are, however, quickly subsumed by other issues, such as the fact that you have yet to unearth, like a neurotic archaeologist, the few bits of meat that are on the dirty plate, underneath the generous heap of ghost chillies.

Ghost chilly, as I prefer to call it, is an exact translation of *bhut jolokiya* in Assamese and Nagamese, also called Naga chilly. While I cannot say with accuracy which part of Assam or Nagaland was its original breeding ground, it is grown in abundance in Upper Assam and the Naga Hills and is hands-down and officially the hottest chilly in the world. There is, apparently a measure for calculating hotness, and this little guy, sometimes green, other times red, is like Superman on steroids on this scale. It *burns* you, man. It sears your soul and scalds your tongue for a week.

While negotiating this degree of hotness unprecedented outside of the legendary Kingfisher Calender and Saturday evenings at the Legends of Rock Café in Bangalore, you will then reach the next level of the game, namely: what is all this oil doing here?

You see, Naga cuisine is either dry or with gravy, like everywhere else, but gravy is not oil-based, or rather with very little of it and not of the red-film-on-top which is the icky mark of common or garden Mughlai. Onions are another traditional absence. So when you have all these, and more, you have to reach in and pull the meat out and eat only those bits with something that might be called *roti* in a very broad sense. The only good news here is the presence of rice, which is fine by me. Otherwise, invoke the golden rule and improvise.

So you make a note of that particular joint and avoid it the next time you are in town. Instead, you very cunningly avoid that street altogether, on the excellent premise that such a diabolical establishment would have corrupted the entire street. You find another place. You find a group of rough chairs and tables with the usual one leg short, but these are trifles. You are a traveller, you tell yourself, not a tourist. The food arrives.

It was made in the same kitchen as the earlier one, dude, *and comes on the same plate.* They're all in on it. You can't win.

My mood lifts with the road from Dimapur as the rains ease in the late morning and we climb the 70-odd km south-east to Kohima. I like the look of the Naga Hills: it's distinctive. They are decently high on this, the eastern end, as they rise progressively westward, steep, jagged and thick with all kinds of trees and the best part is the mist, which seems to hang around the corner all the time and rolls in and livens things up. You do not need to worry about the road because these are specialist drivers, and though the way is narrow, I have never yet seen a bus driver who speeds where he shouldn't on this road.

Just before we leave the plains for the last time is a checkpost where non-residents' Inner Line Permits are checked but which I laugh away easily, and is a personal high point since I became a journalist . . . Yes?

Ed.: Sigh. Nothing. Carry on.

The road to Kohima is being repaired and has already become better. The Border Roads Organisation (BRO) makes good—if narrow—carriageways, but compensates for this with some of the most excruciating road signs you might have ever read. 'Slow drive long life' is sad enough, here's another one, seen every half km: 'It is not a rally, enjoy the valley'.

There is a particularly bad stretch on the Lahaul-Leh road in north Himachal Pradesh, just after the incredibly beautiful Kunjum La Pass. This stretch does not see much traffic, as you might expect, but when it does, gets heavy vehicles like military and civilian trucks and the very occasional civilian off-roader. In winters this road is a nightmare because it is extremely hard to widen into the hard rock of the mountain, and avalanches are common. The BRO, when we were travelling there, had apparently given up trying to fix it sometime earlier and put up this sign instead: 'Sorry for ooh, ahh, ouch, okay?' I suppose it was an ultimatum to accept their apologies or something. I wonder when civic bodies elsewhere (if their reps ever went to such an out-of-the-map place) will borrow this tactic and sort of demand that we get along with bad infrastructure. Or perhaps we have gotten used to it by now.

The first one-third or so of the drive is along a very steep gradient, so the vegetation turns evergreen very quickly and there are pockets on the road where the temperature dips very quickly. If you're on a state transport bus, the window might not close properly, in which case if it isn't raining already and you are not drenched you will feel the bite of the wind. For my co-passengers, none of whom are from the plains, this is usual, but you have to get used to sudden temp differences and cold pockets: they're sometimes a bit of a shock.

Half-an-hour before Kohima comes the one place you must never miss on the narrow road. The Hungry Hop Naga Hotel of Kiruphema is where every early-morning bus stops before the last leg. It is a sinister name. Why would a tea joint refer to a ravenous beer ingredient? What, you muse, would have caused the hop to be hungry? For that matter, what is its preferred diet, just to be on the safe side? Or does it allude to a hopped-up Naga who is hungry? We do not know and sadly we might never find out, because neither the man nor his daughter at the shop know.

The tea is like nothing else you have ever tasted and if you finish it I owe you dinner. The place is a tin shack, as all places here are and the cakes look like really mean two-day-olds. The best combination is to get an unexpired pack of chips from the *paan* shop nearby and sip as little of the tea as possible, but be ostensible in your appreciation to avoid offending the owner who is a very polite man. All this is made up for by a magnificent view of the outer Kohima Ridge because the Hungry Hop sits over the steepest face of a gigantic amphitheatre of mountains. Get used to good views in this part of the world. I check into the seediest hotel I can find near the Nagaland State Transport (NST) terminus in Kohima. It provides only the barest minimum and you have to cart the water from a common washroom to the individual rooms, a bucket at a time. Water is always a hassle in the mountains, with barometric pressure and all. This creates the problem of clean public spaces. In the pre-plastic age, hill towns used to be squeaky clean unless they were near dusty plains. This was never a problem in the region, but ever since plastic came in, streets got a little trash-prone.

What with the temperature pockets and the dry air, you might discover that your skin has gone and died on you, so take suitable measures if you're bothered by that.

Hotels such as the one I am in do not go much for room service. Maybe once a day or in two days, some cleaner might mistakenly knock on the door and sweep the floor a bit, or someone might refill the water jug, but that's it. However, these hotels are low-key and great for watching humanity go by.

By this point, the Cid is in full travel mode. The guy

who won't budge an inch to go out for the evening after work is gone and this one is full of bustle and activity and ideas. Why? Because there is something new to do, something new to see, something more to gain, some more substance to pack between the ears.

The Realm of Crappy Food is behind us, hallelujah and all that. This is where the real fun begins. I have an excellent, slightly spicy, lunch of beef curry with rice, dal and boiled cabbage. They don't go much for experiments with veg food in these parts. Veg is boiled and there's no masala. All the attention is on meat. Okay by me, and boiled cabbage, I think, tastes much better than anything else you can do with it.

Fermented soybeans and yam leaves are two eternal favourites and a regular part of a lot of dishes. You have beef curry in yam leaves, known hereabouts as *akhuni*, with sticky rice and boiled cabbage on the side, paradise.

Kohima is hundreds of years old, and dates back to the time of the rise of the Angamis. There are 15 major Naga tribes in Nagaland, Angamis are one of them. As with other tribal nations, the fortunes of these tribes have varied over the years, with one tribe dominating at some point, and another at a different period. Southwestern Nagaland is Angami area, and Keuhira, a village, was established on the spur of a ridge by an Angami chief from whose name the village was drawn.

The Brits came in the 1860s and found the climate wonderful, so the commissioner of the Naga Hills set himself up here. This was not without resistance, and the first Commissioner was killed by the Angamis, after which there was the usual round of reprisals and colonial arson.

Eventually, things settled down, the Baptist missionaries helping along the way. Now, observe a bit of etymological prestidigitation carefully here, will you? A villager from Keuhira village was called Keuhimiya by other Angamis. The Brits took this name and applied it to their new hill station, and thus Kohima was named. Got it?

The old Naga village is still there, a short walk downhill, and is actually a part of the town. Downstreet a way is the Fire Brigade Colony where you can have your share of the most delightful insects and slugs you have ever tasted. There are these little stalls where you can choose which type of crawly you want to have and they'll cook it for you. The catches come fresh from villages near Kohima, every day, and the preparations are good, but if you don't like chillies too much you got to tell them first.

Over the next four days, I go on a steady diet of decent beef, excellent pork and good old rice. I am not here to gorge on other stuff, but down at Fire Brigade Colony I have some good fried frogs' legs done in exactly the same way they make fried pork ribs, which you *must* have tasted at some time or the other, c'mon. That is, the legs were fried. I do not know about the fate of the remaining parts of the frogs.

Here I must address a most scurrilous myth which has found many takers, re: Nagas eat dogs. This is not wholly true.

Back when the tribes used to rule themselves and good ole animism was the religion, the dog was highly revered. In their mostly hunter-gatherer society, the tribes saw much to respect in the dog: its strength, agility, hunting powers, stamina, speed and, most of all, its loyalty. They treated it very special: you could say the dog was a god for them.

To obtain its qualities and many virtues, to internalise them, in a way, some tribes used to eat dogs in a ceremonial feast. But only a few tribes followed this. Others revered the dog but would not eat it except on very, very special occasions. For yet others, eating such a special creature was, actually, taboo.

So, you see, different tribes reacted in different ways to the matter of the dog.

Young Nagas today travel outside to study and work, and from their culinary tastes this whole idea has come about that Nagas eat dogs as a rule. But these young Nagas, like young people from other cultures, cannot be said to follow their traditional practices, just as there are many Hindus who eat beef as a course, and many Muslims eat pork.

But back at home, traditional Nagas follow their individual tribal customs, and in fact a lot of young Nagas elsewhere do, too. There are people who will walk away when their fellow Nagas plan to snack on a canine, either because it is taboo or because it needs to be a proper ceremony. So there are different degrees of acceptance. Kohima is at an altitude of about a thousand metres, which is just perfect. It is not too low to make you feel you've strolled up a mere hillock, and it's not too high to leave you gasping for breath. The air is particularly bracing and at all times there's a gentle breeze through the streets that really fixes you up. Small wonder the Brits loved it. Sometimes the mist comes down from Mount Japfu, the second-highest peak in the Naga Hills, a short distance from the town, and runs up and down the streets and through the windows, and everything gets hushed, muted. Walking through this kind of mist feels like floating on bits of cloud. The town itself runs up and down a line of hills and looks, if you climb high enough, like bits of building and shacks and ribbons of road strewn over the hillsides.

Back just a while, there was not much traffic in the place, except on the main road to Imphal, which during the day is always full of trucks. Most other places you wanted to reach in Kohima were just a short walk away. Even today most people prefer walking because it is a far less monotonous exercise than in the plains, but there are cabs and such if you don't feel like going uphill. The roads, well, they could be fixed some.

I go to the Kohima War Cemetery, the largest of its kind in these parts. A great battle was fought here during the war, and the cemetery houses about 1,300 Allied dead. The names of those from the Royal Welch Fusiliers (which saw a lot of action), Assam Rifles (which did, too) and elements of the British Indian Army are inscribed on plaques. The graves are in neat rows. You get some kind of idea why they call it a World War when you read the names on these plaques and think of the different corners of the world they came from to this place they had possibly never heard of before. Amuoyi was from the West African Engineers and was killed in August 1943. I do not know which country he was from or his age and I can't pronounce his name, but his grave is next to H. Popper of the Essex Regiment, who died at thirty-one, a year later. Popper was a Jew, as his grave shows. He lies next to E.A. White of the

Royal Welch Fusiliers and B. Beard of the Queen's Own Cameron Highlanders, both presumably Anglicans, but I doubt any of them bothered about this during the fighting on Kohima Ridge over those three terrible months.

Next to these is the grave of an unidentified soldier whose marker says 'Known Unto God'. This was created by Rudyard Kipling when the Commonwealth War Graves Commission brought him on board to help design their graves after the First World War. He wrote the phrase in honour of his son Jack Kipling who died on the first day of fighting at Loos in 1916 and whose body was never found.

Atop the highest level of Garrison Hill is another Crusader sword-cross, this one the grandfather of the one I saw at the much smaller cemetery in Guwahati. Its base is hollowed with stone benches where kids on dates sit and talk (presumably) of love among the remains of their coevals who died over seventy days of bitter fighting on this hill. The cross marks the tennis court of the then Commissioner, where the worst of the fighting took place. The lines of the court are cemented to preserve the place. I sit on an overhang and look out across the city beneath. This is one of those must-listen-to-music moments but I cannot listen to the prelude from *Siegfried* because I left my notebook in Digboi with my folks, this being a cunning insurance measure in case of hassles down the road. Loss of life and limb: unavoidable if things go downhill. Damage to camera: possible, but again understandable. Damage to camera *and* notebook when at least one can be preserved: disastrous.

The bit of sun that has been making various attempts at

appearing over the town vanishes suddenly and things go really quiet. At first the traffic sounds from the Imphal Road downhill get drowned out, then the voices of these three lunatic tourists from somewhere who have also chosen today to climb up to the cemetery and are mucking about two levels beneath me. Cause to celebrate, I tell myself, seated cross-legged on the last stone wall above the drop from the cross to the third level. Then the voices of the couples within the cross's pedestal get muted as well and before I can get a hang of it a heavy bank of mist closes in and blots out the world. I am totally alone in a sea of white tendrils. I can't see more than three feet ahead of me but this is no dadgum use because there is nothing to see at all, except a patch of grass next to the bit of stone wall on which I sit. This is like uber-surreal, man. I mean I know exactly where everything is but they might as well have gone away in a flash. So I hop to the programme, rewind *Siegfried* in my head and listen to 25 per cent of the awesomest piece of music ever made, which must have been created for places like this.

I visit the Art and Culture Department for area maps and the Tourism people and some places of note where I take a look at various things about Kohima's history that I feel are interesting. The few times I have been here in the past have been as a reporter, so those had been simple professional trips with clinical interactions and barely much time on my own to soak in the actual place. Reporters have dual vision, y'see. On the trail of any story they tend to focus on only the intro and the body of the final product they will eventually file, thus pushing to the back of their minds all the other things they might note about a place (possibly for *other* stories afterwards). The second, normal, everyday vision is kept for when they are not on duty though the first thing you are taught in journo school and the last instinct you gain out on the field is you are never, ever, off duty. However, I am, so I mean to look into the culture of the different Naga people.

Kohima Museum is a squat solid-looking building on top of a steep climb down about two kilometres from the centre of the town. At the edge of the cliff on which it is built is the rusting hulk of a Japanese mortar, complete with serial number and other details on the barrel.

Inside, the museum is a three-storeyed treasure chest of all the Naga tribes. On a wall in the lobby is a big chart with the names of the major tribes. The Tangkhul tribe is conspicuously absent. More about this in a bit. On the ground floor and basement are display cases and scale models of Naga houses, clothes, everyday objects and weapons of every description, authentic, antique or especially made by craftsmen for display. There is also—and ye *God of War* people make a note here—a real genuine 100-per-cent hand-cured, man-length shield made of freakin' elephant hide under big display lights which kind of bring out every pore and wrinkle on the grey skin. That shield, which is the biggest one in such superb condition I have ever seen, is *more than an inch thick* even after the taxidermist was through with it and the shieldmaker compressed it to make it even more armoured. In short, the Nagas, when they felt the need for shields after making some of the longest, heaviest and meanest machetes they could find, went, with typical ingenuity, for the most heavily-armoured animal they knew in their world and borrowed its hide. Man, I want I want I want.

The only shortcoming at this wonderful (and mercifully uncrowded) museum is the staff. It has actually got a very small staff, but you will never find them. The only people you will find are from the Culture Department which has offices upstairs. These people are not here to show you around, no sir, nor explain about their culture which, logically, is exactly what you'd think their department is for. They will also not guide you through their archives which they guard tightly for some reason I have never understood. Perhaps it is a secret bank vault. Perhaps the Culture Department recruits the only rude and dense people in the whole of Nagaland. Maybe they go out looking for congenital imbeciles, in an Arkham Asylumesque parody of the search thingy they do for the reincarnated Dalai and Panchen Lamas in Tibet, and bring back infants of promise, who they then feed on a regular diet of dried yam leaves and Dimapur restaurant takeaways until they are grown-up enough to carry the tradition forward.

Peihau Nsarangbe, who has immediately made history by becoming the first friend in this here story whose full name I have given, is an instant exception (hence the Cid's unique way of honouring him). Peihau is Research Assistant at the Museum and nominally attached in some ways with the Ministry of Culture, but he sits here mainly because he is like very few academics I have met. He is really interested in his subject, knows where each file and document is, goes out of his way to bring them out for you and really you do not need it because he knows practically everything about the town, the tribes and the land, and is happy discussing them with you when he evidently has better things to do.

He listens to my crazy ideas about why the Indian National Army should not have rooted for the Japs, agrees mildly when I tell him (rather pompously, in hindsight) that I will not visit the place where Netaji Bose gave a speech back during the siege of Kohima, and then gives me a set of facts and stuff I hadn't known about the war. If you happen to be at the Museum one of these days, look him up because he is indispensable. Chances are the Culture Department has meanwhile detected this unseemly anomaly and posted him to teach culture to the Sangtams, or he's been poached by some big-name university somewhere, but you might just get lucky.

The best part about operating in Kohima, for me, is Nagamese.

All 15 tribes have major linguistic variations, so communication among them was a problem in the past. Eventually they devised Nagamese. Technically, it is a composite of Assamese and a few common words of Naga dialects and Hindi, but an Assamese gets by just fine. The accent is rougher and more angular than the Assamese spoken in Upper Assam, and the grammar defiantly informal in keeping with the Naga attitude, but readjusting takes only a few hours.

Of course there are exceptions. For some time after I hit Kohima I feel like a tennis player against an especially crafty opponent, having to switch the racquet hand as fast as the shots are placed. In some places I find myself switching rapidly from Assamese to Nagamese to English to Hindi in just trying to find out which one they are more comfortable with. In a PCO I try all four in rapid succession, and the woman and, I guess, her brother, shake their heads. In the end I throw up my hands and ask in Nagamese what language they would prefer communicating in. They say English, but getting through is a problem because they use it their way. These are among the few exceptions. Otherwise I am pretty much at home and this is one of the most important reasons why, next to Shillong, Nagaland towns have more Assamese than any other place in the hills.

There is a very special feeling you get when you speak your mother tongue in a different land, perhaps in a different accent or with a few grammar rules bent here and there, but it's the language you know alright. There are too few Assamese in other parts of India to make this a regular, predictable occurrence. Once in a while in the big city you might hear a snatch of conversation and realise the people next to you are from back home, but these are exceptions. Nagaland is the only other place where you get that special feeling of never having left the valley in the first place, and this adds to the experience.

Back in the day the two peoples used to be a lot closer, but this tradition has been fractured of late by Nagaland's encroachment into pockets in Assam. Naga settlements keep coming up in different parts of east Assam and Karbi Anglong, and occasionally there are clashes between locals and encroachers. Whose land is it exactly, perhaps neither state governments know, but they have gone to the Supreme Court over this, I recall, though I dunno what happened. Meanwhile, both state governments actively encourage their people to claim the land for their own.

On the phone a very close friend, S., whom I have promised to update wherever I reach (and who, incidentally, was the same guy I'd rashly promised not to do anything extralegal on this trip), tells me not to go on to Myanmar because of the cyclone. I tell him it's okay: that was down south, that this is a big country and things will be okay in the parts I shall be visiting. I am going to Myanmar hell or high water, the Cid tells himself later. He hopes he is convinced. This part of the country makes its own rules and sometimes you just have to lie low and adjust accordingly.

Over the next four days, I walk through the town, taking pics of the huge All-Tribes Catholic Cathedral. Nagaland, as I think I've said already, is mainly Baptist, but Catholic ministries opened up after Independence and have their flock. The cathedral is built to gigantic proportions with a beautiful red roof and an impressive altar inside. Outside is a big spread of beautiful lawns with paving stones set seemingly at random. But everything has a pattern to it, if you know how to look. From up in the sky, these paving stones form a titanic cross.

The cathedral has a story of its own, too. Sometime back, the relatives, descendents and survivors among the Japanese soldiers who were in Kohima had come over to see the land in which tens of thousands of their people had died. They travelled all over the hills and even met some Naga survivors. These Japanese then contributed money along with local citizens to build this cathedral as a mark of penitence and a way of moving forward from the cataclysmic events of back then. There is a comparatively modest marker behind the cathedral with a message in English and Japanese from the Naga and Japanese contributors for those who come afterwards. It is gestures like these, and cemeteries like here, that narrate more than tellings and retellings of the war years, in evolving towards a world where such events might not happen again. But very few people have the patience to learn, innit?

I do a deal of walking from one hill spur to the other, over the roads which are sometimes decent and other times, well, intractable. This is not an easy country for a walk or even a hike. You climb, that's what you do. The inclines are steep and the hills are, as I said, jagged and crowded with pine and good oak. The roads undulate like little ribbons across the hillsides. Sometimes it rains and the windchill goes up, soaking you from the inside out, but climbing in the rain is a good way to start a day any time.

The best part about the shape and mass of Kohima Ridge is, if you keep an eye closed (but *not* while walking) you can imagine it without the straggle of houses and shacks built into the slopes and just see the land. This great swath of free space, on a non-misty day, makes you feel like you are in one of those sniper simulation games because here, in the clear air and sharp hill lines, you can make calculations about distances, angles and gradients and later walk to and climb just to verify. This is one never-failing way of keeping yourself entertained. With a bit of practice you can get things right to within a few degrees or yards. In short, this is natural sniper country. Do I hear the gentleman at the back ask why? Entertainment, as I mentioned, sir, pure entertainment that you make up as you go along. Livens things a bit.

An eye estimation will tell the visitor that women come out in equal number to men on the streets here. Unlike other towns, where women are concentrated around offices and colleges or similar places, they are found in trade as well here, similar to Imphal and to some extent Shillong. Unlike Khasis, who are matriarchal, some Naga tribes are matrilineal but not matriarchal. These are good strong women used to a sensible approach to anything and getting things done.

The hotel I have picked is distinctive in its seediness, so there is a guarantee of some kind of event here sometime. There is a steady flow of all sorts of people. As I pay another day's rent one evening, three boys come in with three girls. The girl behind me on the left is a professional. How do I know? I know.

They get drunk at night and raise a ruckus during dinner, and as I go up after yet another highly satisfying round of beef, one of the boys is having an argument or something with the professional, sitting at the base of the stairs. She is drunk and clutches the end of my jeans as I step upstairs. The boy gives me the look.

I mentioned that it is important to keep a low profile in new places. Not drinking is important, and so is catching the wind as it changes. Things here reek of alcohol and aggression so I need to fly low and send a quick message to these two. I give the dude the look back which says none of my business and I am not interfering, so don't get ideas. Imagine if I am tipsy as well and a situation develops. Wouldn't want that. The boys are carrying switchblades, which is puzzling.

The Nagas have had insurgency practically since India's Independence, first under the Naga National Council of Angami Phizo, then under the boys of the two NSCNs.

There has been a ceasefire since 1997 but their writ still holds. Another group, the NSCN (Unification) has been active lately.

The rebels, over the years, have enforced a strict form of law and order, and ordinarily petty crimes–especially against or among Nagas—used to bring down the wrath of the rebels something quick. So Nagaland's crime rate has always been very low. These small-time boys with their cheap switchblades, swaggers and wild-eyed attitudes are a rare sight. Perhaps, in the years of the ceasefire, unorganised crime is rising in these parts, which is not good news for anybody, local or outsider.

Overall, however, the town is beautiful and peaceful during my stay. The shops close early and the hotel locks down at 7 pm, a legacy of the decades of strife. They compensate by opening at dawn. It's a different trade cycle and everyone's used to it.

I sleep every cool night and have been breathing easier since I came here. My left lung hurts much less than in the plains. The sound of the professionals and the boys, quarrelling over beer and local rock music in the corridor outside, becomes routine.

Hmm. Kohima is an excellent staging point for all the different parts of Nagaland. Each part is as different as humans can be, so one cannot be seen to the exclusion of the rest.

Consider Khonoma, for instance, at a mere 20 km or so from here, a part of Angami heartland, but with its own story. It has a special place in the history of Nagaland and of the Angamis, because this is where they made their last stand against the Empire in 1879, and no mean feat it was.

A lot of the few foreigners who visit Nagaland make it a point to drop in at this historic site, which began to give its residents ideas.

A while back, the people of Khonoma, making what amounts to a PowerPoint presentation to themselves about the economics of the tourism business, decided to combine their way of life with everything touristy: in short, all the mod-cons.

They began by sprucing up their ancient ceremonial entry gate, tightening the already highly-regarded Naga reputation for hospitality, and building houses in their own style but made for comfortable stays for plainsfolk. They followed this with a voluntary pledge to stop hunting in the forests nearby *and* to protect the trees and animals.

An unsuspecting, but, I believe, happy beneficiary of said idea is a dinky bird called the Blyth's Tragopan, which was till then giving up the ghost and preparing to leave for the Great Aviary In the Sky. In a matter of years, the eco-system was so robust and flourishing that the government, which someone woke up and showed what the villagers had done, gave its *sarkari* red-taped seal of approval and set up the Tragopan Sanctuary.

But the villagers were on to it. They were real clever in their way, so as soon as the Sanctuary was announced, they made an announcement of their own, appointing a village committee to administer and manage it. This has, as I discovered, inspired other self-administered ecological zones in the state.

Wokha is about 90 km almost due north from Kohima, in the hills of the Lotha. The place and nearby areas are best seen on foot, so a good time to visit is autumn, to avoid the rains because walking might be, er, a slippery business, and before the real winter cold has set in. Also because it is such a naturally colourful place that autumn sort of brings it out even more. You will find vast terraced fields of orange and pineapple, the main produce here. Wokha pineapples are like a close second-best I have ever tasted, next to those in southern Mizoram.

You want to pick an orange or something from a plantation? Go ahead, although it is considered polite if you ask the owner first, and he will be happy to let you pick as many as you like or even invite you to lunch and tell you a story.

About three-and-half-hours' walk from Wokha town is Mount Tiyu, where the spirits of the Nagas used to go back in the day. It is a relatively easy incline to negotiate but if you are the sensitive kind and don't much like the idea of a Naga ghost popping up behind you and asking how his pineapple orchard is doing in the hands of his nitwitted great-grandson-in-law, you might make the trip during the day. I'm not saying it happens, I'm just making what they call a speculative statement here.

Places such as Riphyim, about half the distance from Wokha and easily done, also have tourist lodges where you can stay the night. The food is divine, as usual. Since you are here, you might as well see the famous rock bridge of Yikhim, associated today with a relatively recent legend in a land of very ancient tales. Y'see, this was the very same bridge from which a hunter dude jumped on the last living elephant in Nagaland and brought it down with what must have been a very sharp spear. Spurred by the newer fame of Khonoma down south, the Yikhimites say they don't hunt anymore, and instead retell the rock bridge hunt with a lot of relish, with the elephant growing in size each time.

Officials, however, say that elephants have returned to these parts from Golaghat due west of here, and they seem to be staying, so perhaps this part is true. I mean, if someone was hunting elephants in Yikhim, other people would hear of it, wouldn't they? Rather hard to hide that kind of a kill, I think.

Saddle up, peoples, and take the oranges with you if you like, but we must get moving, because the next stop is my favouritest part of a wonderful land. We're going to Ao land, in the deep northern hills.

The steep hills of the Lothas become milder on the about 90 km-long road to Mokokchung, the heartland of the most ancient of the Naga tribes. Mokokchung today is like Kohima, but the real distinction lies about two hours away on foot at Ungma village, where you will find traditional Ao artifacts and thingies if you are into anthropology.

You like gardens? A couple dozen kilometres from Mokokchung is the village of Mopungchuket. Here, virtually every small house has its own garden with beautiful flowers tamed from the wild and of such an absolute abundance of colours that you'll, and I can bet anything here, come away with seedlings and such. Next to it is Awatsung Lake which is particularly beautiful under a winter sun. Another place you must not miss is Chuchuyimlang down the road from Mokokchung to Amguri in Upper Assam. This is officially a model village, and has the added plus of a remarkable experiment.

Y'see, back in the 1950s, a Gandhian named Natwar

Thakkar was sent here by an organisation that worked among tribes. His mission was to organise the village along the Gandhian lines of self-sufficiency on local produce. I'd interviewed him once, a few years ago, and, boy, was it some story.

It wasn't easy adjusting to hill life, particularly back then, and he had had a few unpleasant encounters with militants during what were the red-hot raging days of the Naga rebellion. He even lost a finger. But he kept at it, working with the locals on bee-keeping, farming and marketing the produce. They made that village the pride of the Ao Hills.

The best place to walk in these parts is Kupza, though, a usually level 12 km down a narrow and often muddy rut off the highway, through piney and arrow-straight woods, though there are a few deciduous trees and shrubs too on the way. Here you will find an authentic, traditional Ao village. Every structure is made of wood and on stilts, which was the traditional custom.

But this is not the end of the line, not hardly, because we are going to the highlands: the hills of the Konyak, even more to the east from Mokokchung, another nearly 150 km. There are more Konyaks east of the border, in northern Myanmar, but Mon will have to suffice for now. Occasionally, on this road which can't seem to make up its mind about what it is, an A-grade highway or a village track, to the north you can see the fields and rivers of Upper Assam through the mist.

What? Speak up louder, ma'am, back there. Ahh, you want to know how the Konyaks in Myanmar keep in touch with their people on this side? I see. I will have to take you along to Lungwa village then.

Lungwa sits right in the middle of the international border, making it a marvellous place to visit. Nope, you will not see barbed wire cutting through the place like a clichéd cartoon strip, but it *is* the border, so Lungwa is both here and there, and since it is probably the biggest village in the whole of Mon, there are a lot of houses on both sides.

An even better thing? The chief's house is, y'see, roughly north-south, and half of it is in India, the other half in Myanmar. This is an actual truth, ma'am. If you are well-behaved and know a bit of the customs, you will drop in to say hi to the chief, and he might invite you to his kitchen for lunch, in which case you will be both in India and across simult., thus becoming what may be called an international body. And what a body . . . erm? Oh, nothing, ma'am. Didn't say a word.

Ed.: Hilarious. I get to edit all the wise guys.

The best part is, the headman of Lungwa is in an enviable position, seeing as his jurisdiction is over the entire village and its neighbours in Nagaland, Arunachal and Myanmar, so in effect he sorts out disputes and such in two states *and* two countries, by bilateral agreement, as it were. Name a judge here who can do that, eh?

You cannot have so much power without attendant merits (or depending on your view, demerits) so this headman, he has married what seems to me to be one-third of the eligible women in Lungwa.

You can take walks over the border and visit different people's houses, but do be careful about venturing out beyond the other side of the village into Myanmar. Konyaks get by just fine, but you, my friend, will have to stay within the village *or the bunny gets it.*

This dual existence has meant that the Konyaks are prolly the most intensely independent-minded of all the tribes. This, naturally, led to a split in the NSCN back in the 1980s. While the NSCN (I-M) has people from all the tribes, the NSCN (K), which is just as powerful, is predominantly Konyak and therefore operates as extensively in Myanmar as it used to in India before the ceasefire.

I see I will have to talk about the insurgency a bit here, just to put things in perspective like. But you will have to remember, as I think I mentioned earlier, that not all places in the North-east are disturbed or insurgency-prone. Like other aspects of life here, law and order too is segmented and there are wholly different scenarios in different states. Just because the only time the North-east comes under focus is during a terror strike somewhere does not tar the whole place with the same dark brush.

There seems to be some confusion among you, me friends, about the situation in Nagaland today. In fact, some twit (forgot who, but not among you, I hasten to clarify) wrote somewhere recently about 'the trouble-torn hill-state' or some such. Wake up, man. That's old-story. That's what happens when someone recycles the same overused phrases for a place because there are no fresh updates, no fresh adjectives. That's so dadgum unfair.

See, that's my point. The region is not one complete watercolour of random violence and all kinds of nutcases with demands you wouldn't be bothered to understand. Things change, sometimes for the better, and that is what has happened in Nagaland. To get a clear pic of what exactly happened, then: the short version, which someone here could then pass on to the aforementioned twit.

The Nagas, as I've said, never had a king but all these tribal republics, which kind of didn't get along all the time with one another, but would be damned if they let someone else come in and rule them. They are a proud people. Okay, I mean, who isn't, but considering even the bad ole Burmese back in the early nineteenth century bypassed them on the way to jacking up Assam, they had a point. Till the Brits came along.

The Nagas, naturally, couldn't do much about these new people, but it was always a very tenuous hold the administration had on these hills. I mean, they never really were an easy people to govern, so I don't envy the Brits who went about the villages here for king and country, but always with the suspicion that the benighted natives were waiting for just one chance, just one. Okay, so that was always the case in any frontier hill region, here or near Afghanistan, but the Nagas had their Church and they had British education, so it was much easier for them to learn from events in the west. As it turned out, they were in the middle of world events very soon.

A bit after 1914 came a period that changed this state of affairs, or rather accelerated the way things had been going. Four thousand Nagas volunteered for the British Army and went to France as supply workers behind all that trench fighting going on in those parts just then. The men who returned had seen a lot of the world, particularly Europe, so they had some ideas.

These guys then formed the Naga Social Club, which started out as a reformist kind of unit. These men used to go around to all the villages in the hills, talking to the chiefs and the public, trying to unite all the Naga tribes, because they had realised that, if they were to have any kind of future, they had to stand together.

So by the time the Second World War came around the Nagas were on their way to making decisions as one people. Here occurred the second milestone, something which radically changed the later history of these people from the rest of the region. Point the first, the Japanese invaded India through the Naga Hills. Amid all that destruction and loss of life, the Nagas were reminded once again that only if they were governing themselves could they be safe and avoid being collateral damage in some other nutcase's war.

Point the second, there was a guy, you see, called Zapu Phizo of the Angami tribe, and the moment he saw the Brits being given the almighty smacketh downeth by the Japs, he went to Burma and signed up with the Japs, to try to liberate his people Netaji Bose-style, and for the next three years it could have gone either way.

But, well, that didn't go down too well in the end, as we know, but Phizo made it out of the Burma mess alive. With Independence for India being talked about really seriously by nearly everyone, Phizo decided to do a William Wallace first.

So what he did, he went around talking to *all* the big people in the North-east, counting, from left to right, the Khasis, Garos, Assamese, Meiteis in Manipur, Mizos, like everyone. He had made up his mind to take the whole region out in one gigantic liberation struggle.

Man, that would have been something to see.

As it turned out, other people had a lot of Gandhianism and such going on at the mo, led by Assam, where there'd been some super-huge street protests, marches and whatnot, like the rest of the country. So Phizo was left to take his own people out.

Meanwhile, a delegation of Naga elders went off to meet Mahatma Gandhi, to talk about their people and where popular sentiment really was, namely, to form a separate country. Gandhi met them (I dunno where exactly this took place but I guess this was during one of the great man's fasts in eastern India). Gandhi listened to all the facts as they were placed before him, and being the sort of person he was, agreed that the Nagas, indeed, had a case for independence. In fact, the zigact quote from him on this is something on the lines of: 'Like the Nagas, if any people do not wish to be a part of Independent India, and there is a historical basis for an independent state, it will not be correct to hold them by force.' Man, this is a real quote somewhere.

So the elders went back home, satisfied they had Gandhi's word. What they hadn't reckoned with was he would not be in charge when the stuff hit the air-conditioner. It would be Nehru.

So Nehru visited the North-east a bit after the Gandhi meeting and did a tour, sort of. The elders went to meet again, I think this time accompanied by Phizo, to work out matters, seeing as he would be the Indian Prime Minister and all.

Nehru refused to meet them.

That was effing it for the elders. They had Gandhi *burha*'s (old man) word, so it was to be on these lines. Man, there's a parallel right there with Aung San and the northern Burmese tribes. We'll check that in a while.

So Phizo's men of the Naga National Council declared independence on 14 August 1947, after which, as the great Amazing Ben would put it, 'it was on like neckbone'.

At this point you're going to ask: 'But how were they going to enforce this declaration, in the face of the Indian Army?' Precisely, good question.

Back during the Burma Campaign, the British airdropped like tonnes of arms, ammunition and medical kits all over the Naga Hills. The logic behind airdrops in those days was you didn't need to be precise so long as the soldiers on the ground got as much of the packs as they wanted. Some packs fell into Japanese hands. In fact, people say more Jap soldiers got these packs than the Brit soldiers themselves.

But most of these drops fell in Naga hands.

It was a godsend, seeing the way things were going. These packs were gathered and tabulated by the Naga groups and then safely hidden away. Some were used by small vendetta groups against the Japanese, but most of them were safe and in working condition.

So when the Naga Hills district of Assam (as it was called back then) summarily declared independence and the Indian Army marched in expecting to roll over these guys, they were faced with sub-machine guns, grenades and all manner of pointy assault.

And *that* is how the Nagas started independent India's first rebellion, as it is called. Of course, depending on which side of the debate you are, you can call it any of a number of things, with the benefit of hindsight: insurrection, freedom struggle, militancy.

What it was *not* was easy. The army was fighting on hostile terrain, hostile in all senses of the word, against a tightly-knit, well-trained and determined force armed with the same weapons they had.

So this went on escalating for some time till Phizo met Nehru in Tezpur and Dibrugarh in Assam in 1951 and '52, and even in Delhi that year. Things just didn't work out. In 1954, with all chances of dialogue kind of dying out (whose fault it was depends on, once again, which side of the argument you take) he announced the formation of the People's Democratic Republic of Free Nagaland. That same year, with the Indian Army ratcheting up their operations, Phizo went into exile, ultimately reaching London. He stayed there till his death in 1990, directing the rebels. His son and daughter there still lead the Naga National Council, such as it is.

Phizo's movement was eventually overtaken, not by the Indian state, but by developments in his homeland and the resurfacing of old tribal divides, which can be pretty strong, all things considered.

Y'see, in 1980, a much older Phizo's NNC signed the Shillong Accord with the government, which didn't go down very well with hardliners who wanted like total independence (I think the accord was about some kind of a compromise formula). So the hardliners broke off and formed the National Socialist Council of Nagaland, the NSCN, and went right back to the original rebellion of 1947.

Things kind of continued in this vein for the next eight years, but it seems the leaders were not either as charismatic or determined about a totally united Naga group being the only answer. So differences emerged along tribal lines, leading to the inevitable split.

In 1988, then, the NSCN split into the two groups you might know today. One is the NSCN (I-M), led by Isak Chisi Swu and Thuingaleng Muivah. This group is mainly drawn from the Tangkhul tribe of northern Manipur. Truth is, other Naga tribes don't like the Tangkhul that much, between us. They think the Tangkhul are kind of too smart for their own good and perhaps even influenced by the Manipuris from the plains, culturally and otherwise. So once in a while the other tribes accuse the Tangkhuls of hijacking Phizo's rebellion just so they can lead the rest of the people.

The other group is the NSCN (K), led by S.S. Khaplang, and a general secretary, Kitovi Zimomi. This here group is mainly Konyaks, who as you know are also in northern Myanmar, so they operate on both sides of the border.

The two groups, obviously, don't get along very well with each other, and back when they were still fighting the Indian state they also used to have skirmishes on the side.

However, both groups were heavily armed, well-trained, had excellent working relations with other groups in the North-east (which look to the Nagas as the fountainhead of armed struggle) and with rebels across in Northern Myanmar through intricate treaties.

All this time, the rebels carved out large areas of Nagaland and neighbouring states where they pretty much ran things independent of state control, I mean, taxes, administration, legal matters, the works.

After nearly a decade of fighting, the NSCN (I-M) began a ceasefire and negotiations with the Indian government.

This was followed by the NSCN (K) coming in from the cold too. I-M men are based in camps inside Nagaland.

Isak and Muivah sometimes visit India to talk with the Centre, but, you know, between us, I'll tell you something. The Indian state has been pulling their chain for a while, I mean; the talks have not really progressed much. The Centre's gameplan is that these men are old, okay, so they're sort of tired and prolly wouldn't want to return to the old Violent Marv days.

I mean, what do old men want, really? They look back at their lives, and no matter if they are in Delhi or Kohima or some nice apartment in Antwerp, regardless of their being Naga or Assamese or Indian, they look back at their lives (particularly at night when old men, I am told, find it difficult to sleep) and they think a lot. They ask themselves what legacy they will leave behind, to show that they were there. Isak, Muivah and the rest want to leave behind an independent Nagalim, but they get older by the day. The Centre wants to keep them hanging on to the ceasefire till they pass away, that's what the game is about.

So, who knows? I think, you know, those two men are kind of getting tired that the talks have not progressed to anything concrete. And, as we know, old men can get desperate sometimes. So if the Centre continues this wearing-down policy, I can't say what the future will bring.

But, in short, Nagaland is at peace today, and that's all she wrote. So if you read that there twit and his 'trouble-torn hills' kind of sentence, don't pay much attention to it. The twit doesn't know anything, whoever he is. Times change, and since this is a super-awesomely beautiful land with great hosts as the people, Nagaland is worth a visit any day.

Ahh, I see a hand raised there, at the back.

You want me to explain this word I used back there, is it? Nagalim? You want me to explain that? Okay.

Simply put, Nagalim is the rebels' map of an independent Naga homeland. This covers areas where Naga tribes have traditionally lived and still do today. So this kind of covers the whole of Nagaland, this large chunk off northern Manipur, like nearly half of that state, the whole of eastern and central Assam *nearly till Guwahati*, and about one-third of Arunachal from its east, plus the Konyak bits off Myanmar—and taking *that* out is another task altogether, you can say that.

That there is a powder-keg by itself, because it will decimate the rest of the region. That map is simply *huge*. There is no way the other states are going to agree to it, I mean just the mention of that map causes riots and such, so dialogues with the Naga groups are kind of stuck at this point as well.

Meanwhile, we proceed with the taking-a-look-around part.

Zunheboto, due east from Wokha, is a steep rise through the hills and is where the Sema tribe lives, again totally different from its neighbours. It is mostly high-altitude, between like 1,200 m and 2,000 metres plus, with mist and winds, so it gets cold here, even in summer, so be prepared. Besides the villages and places there is a bit of climbing if you are interested. There is a bunch of caves near Aizhuto, one of which is rumoured to house Satan, Prince of Darkness, et cetera. An interesting sidelight, so if you want to take a look you might have to do some climbing. Tell me what happens when you reach there.

Between Wokha, Zunheboto and the neighbouring

Tuensang are some of the steepest terraced slopes you'll ever find, some so steep that you wonder how any fertile soil ever stays intact during the rains, but it does and there's a lot of intensive cultivation just there.

This whole business of the rains washing away overturned soil each year led to the fashioning of *jhum* cultivation, the broader aspects of which you must have read at school. Basically, a plot of land on a hillside, the part with the most gradual gradient, is cleared of trees, after which the grass and undergrowth are burnt. This not only saves the trouble of clearing out shrubs by hand, but the burnt shrubbage also ends up providing farmers a ready source of fertiliser. There is only a limited window for cultivating this cleared patch before the rains wash all the fertility away, after which another patch is found and cleared. While the farmers move away, the plot gets a breather and gets time to re-grow vegetation and recover fertile soil.

After Zunheboto we reach Tuensang district, again a high-altitude place, going up beyond 2,500 metres with Nagaland's highest peak being one of them, but with some valleys in it and different kinds of vegetation. Whose land is it? you'll ask, seeing as each district belongs to a particular tribe. Truth is, I don't know, because there are nearly ten tribes who live in equal numbers here: Aos, Sangtams, Phoms, you name them. As you go up through the bouncy roads hanging on to your vehicle, you'll go cross-eyed at each tiny village you pass, trying to decide which tribe lives next to which.

My walking around Kohima is done. I would love to stay, but my budget has to be watched over, despite my frugal living, two meals a day and the cheap hotel. I pack once again for the journey down south to Manipur.

ELEVEN

I wake up on day five to a Kohima dawn, rub my hands, partly in anticipation of a long day ahead and partly because it is nice and cold. I take stock of the journey so far.

By air and road, I have clocked 2,542 km through Guwahati, Upper Assam and Nagaland. Despite the rain and the occasionally difficult roads, it has been a smooth ride. The next phase will be completely different. There will be no transport at night, so I will be changing the usual method of night travel. Instead, in the next phase, it will be very important that I make each leg before dusk.

Since this has begun to sound like the prologue to *The Vampire Chronicles*, I got to explain: Manipur, where we are going, is in a bit of a mess and likely to continue that way for the foreseeable future. The best way to reach Imphal is by air, is what people have kept on telling me. However, since I *will* travel by road this time, I need to follow the new rules and be ready for maximum improvisation because there are hardly any road travellers these days from Kohima to Imphal, and definitely no one from the plains. Certainly no one alone.

Damn. Every time you analyse a stage before you start it, and the road looks a bit sticky, you get greatly tempted to change your plans. Particularly in Manipur. But I got to see this through. It is only a matter of less than 90 km from Kohima to Imphal.

So, I am packed and out in the early dawn, determined to reach Imphal before dusk. I walk a huge distance of 20 metres to the Nagaland State Transport terminus, where a drowsy gentleman going off the night shift tells me with suspicious promptness and a certain degree of what I think is ghoulish cheer that there are no buses to Manipur today, nor were there any last week and there won't be any in the days to come. Thus begins that dadgummed road. There are two routes to Imphal by road. One is the Golaghat-Kohima-Imphal road on which I stand. The other drops down from central Assam through our Karbi Anglong hill district to Silchar in south Assam, from where it reaches Imphal. I do not feel comfortable travelling in the Silchar area because the place feels so damn alien. It is perhaps the only place in the world I take great care to avoid. Cultural reasons, thassall. I have never ben able to make much sense of that place, particularly Silchar town itself, although the countryside is beautiful (but out-of-bounds these days because of militants).

So the Silchar route is best avoided, from what I see, and besides, to go down that road I need to return to Assam and that will shave off days from my plans. I must, therefore, continue down this road, but by some other means.

North Manipur people seem to have an economic blockade going on, so buses and trucks are not allowed to pass from Nagaland. This blockade bit has more ins, outs and what-have-yous, as I shall discover shortly. Because each state is dependent on roads passing through their neighbours' for essential supplies, blockades kind of hit the jugular of the state governments, and are thus effective political tools, but that's only the half of it. Along with strikes, bandhs and student unrest, blockades are a bit of a cottage industry in the North-east, and nowhere more than in Manipur, where virtually everything extra-constitutional is a c.i.

Bwahaha, they reckoned without the Cid's ingenuity and remarkable knowledge of how the wind blows. Because at the other end of Kohima is a taxi stand meant just for situations like these. After a few years of blockades in north Manipur, Kohima cabs worked out an arrangement by which they take people to the state border at Maram. Here, the passengers get on another cab from the other direction and continue south. Thus they work around the blockade.

On the Manipur side, the cabs stop at Senapati town in the district of that name, where, till about three in the afternoon, they can get buses to Imphal. But that is the last bus, so in case of delays, passengers are stuck at Senapati.

I therefore reach the other end of Kohima, where at the head of the cab line I get on board a packed Maruti van that will take me some distance across the state line. My co-passengers are Manipuris who either work in or had come to Kohima for short stays and are eaten up from head to toe with curiosity at me. They never get outsiders on this route.

I explain that I am from Guwahati. Saying I work in Delhi would make it a long and complicated story, and, from here on at least, it is better if the people think I am from somewhere in the North-east and travelling on some work. One little old lady on the front passenger seat, on discovering that I have come from Guwahati, tells me that her younger son is at a college there, at some neighbourhood. I know that neighbourhood and I know the college. I can describe the buildings and everything else, but at the moment I just can't remember the name. I reach out wildly and suggest what I think is the correct name, but she is a little doubtful. She can't remember either. Someone tries to fit in a coop of chickens at the back and people make rude remarks about chickens in general.

Public transport is fun anywhere in rural India. There is no end to what people carry with themselves, as is the case anywhere else in the world. Goats come a distant second and vegetables tie with fish as third, but chickens are always lively, once they're fitted on board. Back a long time ago, if some of you remember, there used to be a service called Vayudoot, which used to be mainly within states, or, in the case of the North-east, from one state to another.

So there was this one flight from Tezpur to Itanagar, just twenty minutes or so. It was a small aircraft, maybe twenty passengers, and remember, tickets used to be expensive. People used to make the most of this, and practically every passenger used to carry coops of chickens on board, stashing them under the seats of this decrepit aircraft with cracked windows and fractures on the inner walls. Honest. That plane used to look like it would fall apart the moment it was airborne.

I don't know what happened to that route after Vayudoot went out, but while it lasted, those chickens *loved* the flight.

It is raining heavily now, a squall that's perhaps an after-effect of the cyclone wind movements in the other country.

About three kilometres after Kohima the road does the first of its disappearing acts. There are many such spots I pass on the way, alternating stretches of level metalled surfaces and totally unpaved parts. I have as yet found no logical explanation for this. Why, we ask ourself, must one stretch be metalled and another left out? What is to recommend one part of the road over another? There is hardly any difference between the two spots, is there?

The unpaved parts get eaten away by the rain which washes the soil over the edge and downhill, so they are like huge depressions on the ground, made worse in places where the authorities have piled stones for possible future road-work. Not very easy going. My co-passengers are barely bothered by all this. These two ancient guys on both side of me want to know why I am going to Manipur, and alone, and if I smoke, following which they tell me I should be very careful in Imphal because things are not good. They say it in a way that makes clear they don't know why someone from the outside should be on this road at all. They could have been a bit more cheerful, I mean this is hardly what I want to hear.

Just as we reach Mao, at the Nagaland border, we find the beginning of a big group of stalled vehicles. This should be interesting. These vehicles should be meeting up with those from the Manipur side about half-a-dozen kilometres further south, where the passengers usually make the switch.

But the vehicles are stalled here because, it seems, there is a landslide up ahead and no one is going anywhere. This puts a crimp on everyone's plans. 'Landslide' is a ubiquitous term in the mountains and refers to a whole range of totally unrelated things. Some of these, shall we say, accidents, are totally different from one another, distinguishable by someone familiar with these events, but someone had to club them under a single all-purpose name because it all looked the same to him, therefore the term. But each incident could be different from the other. It depends on familiarity.

Someone once told me that Laplanders have twenty-three different terms for snow. Think about it. There's just two kinds of snow I can think of: fresh and dirty. But some Laplander felt the need for differentiating snow into two dozen types, and who's to blame him? There's a tribe up in Arunachal that has fifteen names for bamboo. They need those names.

So, about landslides. They come in as many sizes as there are things on the hills. A man-sized rock rolls down a hill and dares you to pass–landslide. This is actually a rockslide, and could be just the start of something much worse. But it is easy to detect, when the hillside starts rumbling, giving you some kind of warning.

A trickle of topsoil, tree-trunks and mud wallowing aimlessly on a clifftop–landslide again. This is a mudslide, and far, far more dangerous, because it doesn't make a sound. More people get killed in the mountains under loose mud than under rocks, because nobody takes mud seriously.

There are types and degrees of magnitude for such events. Half a branch of an old alder tree gets bored with life and suicidal and takes a running jump off a hill–you know what it is called. It's just an old branch, but if it falls in front of your off-roader and you get shocked out of your skin you'd think the hills are collapsing around you and you yell landslide.

People get philosophical about such road blockages. Back in Mao, we get out into the rain and rush to stand inside some village stalls. The other passengers look up at the sky and their watches. We haven't made bad time so far; there's a lot of daylight left, so they say they'll wait out till when the road clears. It's the beginning of the monsoons and it had to happen, sooner or later. Some of them know people in this village, so they can fix lunch and such if needed. Others carry their food with them. It is only a temporary problem. At least they are mostly out of the heavy rain.

How bad can it be, I wonder. In a pinch, the locals can shack up at the little village, though it might not take many people. But me, I've got to reach Imphal by dusk. I can't hang around random villages asking if I can stay. No one knows the exact scene up the road or if the slide or whatever it is can be negotiated. They just saw vehicles returning and stopped as well. How bad can it be? The Cid decides to hike it.

I take a handy branch and break it into shape. A walking stick is vital if you are going up a steep incline on an uncertainly-built road with a pack that can throw you off balance.

The numerical-minded pack a footmeter on walks. Another improvisation if you don't have a footmeter is to get one of those clicky things (like they showed on the Ben Affleck Axe ad), tie a knot and loop it down your ankle so that the knot moves up to the clicky thing each time you step forward. A few tests and you can make an almost accurate estimation of how far you have travelled per click. An easier way is to click it, say each 100 steps, after you have estimated how far one step covers.

However, all this is merely for exactitude. You can just as easily get an eye-estimation of the distance you have covered.

I do five easy kilometres uphill before I come across the slide around a loop in the road and see what it exactly is. Obviously, the slide, being a crafty specimen, is waiting around a hairpin for the unwary. Half the hill has rolled down in a cascade of mud and taken away the whole road, the bend and anything else I see beyond it. The hills of the North-east are so green and lush that you would be pardoned for believing they are solid earth. On the contrary, their bones are hard rock, granite and limestone and very old, older than the Himalayas in some places. Actually most mountains are older than the Himalayas, which are made of, as we know, shale (snigger snigger) and ichthyosaur droppings.

Some of these venerable gents have also rolled down the hill. The very contour of the area is altered. The hill on the right is now at an exact ninety degrees. Everything else is gone. This is impressive and if the Cid was not an impecunious walker he would risk the camera for a shot in the rain. Meanwhile, the rain itself has trickled inside my clothes, but it is not very cold, so it is reasonably comfortable. I take in the scene because I need to find my way across and continue down the road.

The last slide I had gone over was one of solid rock on the road to Tabo in HP. It was a forbidding sight with a backdrop of bare rocky mountains and the bodies of four roadcon workers behind us. But it was still not difficult deciding to cross it. As I said, slides are of different types and some are really easy to cross.

The thing with rock is, if the pieces are big and they don't take the level road down with them, they are stable enough for my weight to climb over. The problem with mud, on the other hand, is it shifts. Not quickly, nor with the rumble of good rock, but like treacle, and you never know which way it is going, it is that slow. Given a mudslide and one of rock, I'd take the latter any day. This is a problem. Do I go over or walk back? The road just before was very narrow to begin with, and as the rain fell in greater amounts, the mud became thicker and more difficult to walk in. Going back the five km to where the vehicles are parked is a last option. I walk over to my left, to the cliff edge.

The slide drops straight down about 800 feet. This is eye estimation only: I do not intend (even for you guys) to go down there with or without a measuring tape. It could be less or more. It is also about -50 degrees in gradient. Get it? The slide has hollowed out the cliff beneath the road too. This means the patch of road I'm on is a lot unstable, I mean it could just collapse if any more mud fell on it. It does not look good.

I poke the mud with the stick and step on the slide. The apex is about twelve feet up. I step on rock wherever possible. The mud is sticky and my shoes sink slo-o-o-w-ly into it as I pull up with my left hand. It takes five minutes to the apex, movement is that slow. From here I try to step in a straight line across the top of the pile (note: I am climbing as far right on the slide near the hill as possible, and as much as I can *away* from the drop. I am not suicidal). Five steps on, I check if the earth has moved left. There is no way of making exactly sure but I think it's safe enough. This was such a bad idea. I don't like mudslides, man.

It is one of those times when your mind takes in everything in such clear detail that you wish later that you had such clarity in everyday life. One wishes to be somewhere else, and fast, but meanwhile one notices everything. The rain, the exact feel of mud and rock, the hills all around, the feel of the stick, the uniform greyness of the sky.

I think the mud shifts a little. I cannot be certain about this, but the top of the slide gets narrower towards the end. It drops down to the other side after about a hundred metres. Whoever's going to fix this will need lots of bulldozers and things, and those people back there in those vehicles will be waiting around for a while before they can get across. I step down onto a semblance of a road and walk up the incline again. These are not black-topped roads anymore, but at least they are walkable.

Mucking aound in that mud I have to do a mental check of the few first-aid things I carry. These can come in handy sometimes, particularly when you are on your own and have to do some basic repairwork when needed. A few medicines are usually sufficient, but additional stuff is up to you or the likely scenarios particular to each trip. For instance, you might have to bandage yourself up sometime, or carry fast-acting painkillers or something. Or, just in case, disinfectants and antibiotic vials, for which you'll also need syringes *and* you need to know what they are all about because you wouldn't want to find yourself randomly jabbing your arm on some lonely stretch, makes you look like an idiot, if only to yourself.

If you can make your own stitches and such, carry the specified needle and thread, it's a further add-on which can be of great help, but that is *only* in worst-case scenarios and only on yourself, unless you are a doc and are therefore allowed to practise on other poor chaps. It's good to be prepared, is what I say.

As I walk I feel light, although the pack weighs me down. At least the pack and the camera case are waterproof, but that's like a necessary requirement anywhere you go.

There is nothing like a light pack on your back while walking long distances. You get a lot of mobility that way; your hands are free for balance, and after some time you get used to the weight.

Special forces like the SAS sort of have it mandatory to carry huge backpacks filled with rocks and such on training marches, weighing about thirty-five kilos. Some march it must be. This is not a random figure someone arrived at. This goes back to the old Greek city-states and their citizen soldiers, whose armour and weapons totalled about this weight. And remember they were infantry, so they marched cross-country with all that weighing them down. The contemporary Greek has a beer belly.

More reflections on this strange historical connection as I walk in the rain. There is barely any other noise in the hills. In the distance the terraces of hillside villages are sodden fields.

We borrow a lot of things from really ancient conventions and practices, a kind of continuous system that we don't even know has crept into our lives. I was reading the other day about how the booster rockets for one of those space shuttles have only a fixed payload. This is because the rockets can be only of a fixed diameter, and no bigger.

This, in turn, is because the rockets are transported to the launchpad from their manufacturing site by rail, and their diameter has to be in proportion with the broad gauge tracks. These tracks have been of a specific size ever since railways began. I forget the exact distance between the tracks, but it seems that distance was fixed by early rail engineers about a hundred and seventy years ago.

At this point, then, you'll ask why this particular distance was fixed back in the day. It was because the factories or workmen already had this measure for the axles of horse-carriages, so they just transferred it to the railways because that would be easier to manufacture.

So why was this distance used by horse carriages? Well, it goes back to the first century, when the Romans built roads with grooves cut into them on which chariots could run, and this was the length of the axles on those chariots. But why this length?

Because this was the minimum length into which two Roman warhorses, or rather their behinds, could be fitted under a yoke. In other words, the size of the trains on which we travel, and the size of the rockets scientists build to send space shuttles out there, was fixed by the size of the behinds of horses two thousand years ago.

Face it, man, history plays a more powerful role in our lives today then we care to admit. Things are connected. This is a comforting thought, a kind of continuity. Dunno about you, but I'm okay with it. Hate to think if everything new is wholly unconnected with whatever achievements were made by those who came before us (if this was the case, a thousand years from now people won't even stop to consider what new things our present civilisation created, which would suck something big).

Thinking such random thoughts, eight miles into a very wet but thoroughly satisfying walk, after crossing a place called Maram, I find the other stalled vehicles. I get into another crowded Sumo returning to Manipur. My co-passengers, some of them from Nagaland, give me more creepy advice as they probably do to the almost-extinct stranger in these parts. Be careful in Manipur. Things are bad. Don't smoke in public. Be careful how you talk to people. In fact, don't talk to people. Why are you travelling alone?

The rain eases and becomes a drizzle of sorts. Things are going alright, I say. I haven't been unduly delayed, it has been smooth so far and I feel like whistling. Ever heard me whistle? No? I whistle on my runs. I'm happy. The road climbs down from here towards the plains of central Manipur.

They are waiting around another bend on the road. There are five, some in camouflage, others in jeans and black tees with bandnames and such. Not an impressive-looking bunch from a distance, but everyone knows what they are carrying in their hands. This had to happen in this area.

They flag down the van and talk to the driver in Manipuri. From what little I understand of the language, they're asking the usual questions about where everyone's going and so on. Mainly, it's to check if outsider-owned vehicles are running on these roads, which is not allowed. Local transport vehicles pay taxes to them. They talk through the windows with my co-passengers in Manipuri. Then they look at the only non-Manipuri in the car. They make me get down. Their boss, who is the oldest among them and looks twenty, carries a carbine. Three others carry pistols or revolvers. The fifth has his hand inside the pocket of a sleeveless jacket and I guess is holding a Chinese lever-action grenade, very common in these parts and with an awesome reputation of seldom going off. It is a thought, nevertheless.

The boss looks stoned to his eyebrows and so do his boys. They make me walk a bit up ahead to the edge of the road. Then he reverses the carbine and hits me on the ribs with it. Then he does it again.

If it were my left side I would have gone down. As it were I feel my right bruising and my insides jarring. I suppose the blows are meant to buy him time to frame questions because eventually he asks me in English: 'Where are you going, brother?'

The rest of the conversation is slow as I explain, using as short words as possible, about everything, mainly that I am a humble traveller on a humble journey. I do not tell them that I am going to Myanmar because they'd ask me why, and what I know of the place, and it would come out that I am familiar with the area, which would lead to more uncomfortable questions. I try to be as contrite as possible. Poor Cid. Wretched Cid. Misbegotten planner to have travelled the narrow road to this drizzle and this junkie militant who pokes me with the carbine barrel on the left shoulder with each word. (Course I don't tell them this in so many words.) They really don't care about my i-card or that journalists are off-limits. They've gotten so used to local journos being mixed up in their business that the press does not really mean anything different to them than yet another employer. I won't get a break because of my profession. The rules don't work except when they see fit to apply them.

Let me tell you a small something here. I am always afraid, like a lot of people I know. If it isn't of reaching late for an assignment, it is for turning in shoddy copy or not meeting often enough with friends or missing lunch and dinner. Or a mudslide. Or being shot in the rain. I suppose you would think less of me now. I am not fearless. I haven't yet known anyone who is, although once in a while you'd meet people who make such claims. But I know I shall start worrying when being afraid stops me.

As I explain I realise how unlikely the whole thing sounds even to myself—why I am here, where I am headed for, travelling on my own. It takes half-an-hour but they eventually conclude that I am no danger to their Peoples' Liberation. They ask what is in the pack and camera case but don't make me open it.

In a lifetime packed with idiotic mishaps, I have been at the wrong end of a gun on a few occasions. I swear this won't be the last of them. What worries me, however, is that the boy has his finger inside the trigger guard all the time. And you know the other thing I realise just then? I might have medicines and such in my bag, but guess what I did not bring with me? Celox. Eventually they let me go, and it is kind of weird because they don't even extort money from me. They usually don't let go of a chance to earn a bit.

They also don't take away my camera, though they must have guessed it from the bag, which is a lucky, lucky thing. Overall, I get away considerably more easily than usual. I travel to Senapati in an awkward silence. The other passengers seem to think I am infected or otherwise a kind of militant-magnet, like merely by being on this road I was asking for trouble, which, in their eyes, is prolly a reasonable suspicion. My ribs ache something bad.

Senapati district is north of and adjoining Imphal. Here the hills roll down into narrow valleys with cultivable swathes of land. This area and north of it has a lot of the Tangkhul Naga tribe. I am told that the last bus to Imphal leaves Senapati town at 3:30 in the afternoon. The other passengers say we are going to make it, just barely. I hope we do. The idea of hanging around outside Imphal at night is definitely not a good one.

Of course we don't make it. We reach to see the tail-end of a very crowded bus disappearing at the other end of the town. I am told to put up for the night, and quickly. Things are bad here. The other passengers just vanish into their friends' or relations' houses. The blockade has gone up several notches in temper.

It seems at some point the people of North Manipur discovered that there were practically no teachers in government schools here. They racked their brains and came up with a wholly original idea: economic blockade. They stop all public vehicles and don't allow them to pass to Imphal. Back in Dimapur I had found stacks of undelivered goods in transport agents' offices, marked 'Imphal'.

These goods were awaiting trucks back into Assam and down through Silchar, the other route into Manipur. But some trucks continue through Nagaland to the Manipur border. Here they haul up and stick together till the government makes arrangements for them. Some of the trucks manage to reach the capital in convoys with paramilitary protection of sorts, because they don't want to be torched by the locals along the road. I totally don't want to waste time here in Senapati, which also does not have any hotels. I had said I was going to Myanmar hell or high water. High mud was over, and so was a small bit of junkie hell. What more could happen?

When in a serious crunch, you've got to access the authorities and make them work. I usually do not like asking them for help and such. They have attitude problems, they don't understand why anyone should be travelling at all and they act pricey if they find you need their help, particularly in remote areas. In this case, however, I need to get things moving if I am to get out of Senapati.

I cross the road to the local police station where I find a lone truck from Guwahati, manned by Manipuris, waiting for the evening convoy. I talk to the cops (who *also* express surprise that I am travelling alone and without security in these parts, man these reactions are becoming such a bore) and tell them how important it is that I get some way out of there. They walk me over to the truck, where we talk to the people inside and I hitch a ride with them. The truckers also want to know why I am alone but they seem a friendly type and don't mind making some room for me inside. Back across the road I lunch on pork curry and rice on a dirty plate (I haven't seen a clean plate in ages) at a rundown restaurant, up behind a line of shops, on a terrace cut into the earth. That restaurant, peoples, is run by the most beautiful waitress I have ever seen. Seriously. The restaurant is called Manipur Hotel and is opposite the police station, in case any of you happen to pass by there sometime and want to verify things.

Now, don't get me wrong, I don't go about ogling women. This is only aesthetics, alright? Excuse me, the gentleman at the back again.

What, you want to see her pics? Sure, and her husband at the counter paring something or the other with a whacking great *dao* would have posed for me too. Sir, I am glad I do not travel with you.

The boys in the truck are refreshingly friendly and I get along fine as they rev up when the convoy rushes through town and does not even slow on its way. There is very little time till dusk. We join it towards the tail. It's a long line of trucks and Sumos. Dusk falls as we try to reach Imphal on time before everything closes. My worry is to get a hotel for the night in that town. We cross the plains of Senapati.

Trucks have a spartan attitude to seating and such. Sometimes the driver might have a thin rug or something over the seat, whose cushion would have long ages past been knocked out. There is, particularly in older trucks, another cushioned seat out in front, but most truckers pull that out for easier access, because, particularly in areas like the North-east, truckers travel in groups of four or more per truck, unlike the usual two. Safer that way. So pulling off the front passenger seat makes it easier to fit more people in, and for getting on or off.

Behind these two seats there is usually a flat plank lined

up against the rear wall of the cabin. Under this is a compartment where they keep their clothes and such, and being directly above the gearbox, it gets hot in summers. On this plank, in my truck, there are three other guys. Sitting on a rough wooden plank on the kind of road we are on is, to make a very large understatement, not exactly comfortable.

They tell me their stories. They started from Guwahati before they heard of the blockade, and by the time they reached Dimapur, the owner back in G. told them to keep going. But they missed out on the earlier convoy and were kind of forced to wait for the next one at the police station. The owner does not really care what happens to them so long as the truck and the consignment are safe and in Imphal on time.

The truck malfunctions a bit. They get down and fix it, there's a bit of tinkering under the bonnet and round about the axle. We have stopped at a potholed stretch between two long stretches of rolling fields. The setting sun shines off the beige-green hills of Senapati. There isn't any habitation around or people and of course no traffic coming the other way. Meanwhile, the convoy does not wait because it has its own schedule to run. Way I see it, there is hardly any protection for the two-dozen trucks and such from the six paramilitary vehicles and lightly-armed soldiers. They're just there same as during those flag marches they hold in towns after riots or during curfews, a show of implied strength and such. The blockade, remember, is by civilians, so any guess if the paramilitary will use force against civilians in a pinch in an area already hostile to the government? Didn't think so.

So when the convoy leaves us behind we are left to our own devices. Return to Senapati or keep going and try to catch up with the others? The second is an easier option, but it's kind of difficult to speed on a road like the one we are on, so I doubt we'll rejoin the convoy anytime soon.

It is dusk by now and we are approaching the southern end of Senapati district when we see torches in the distance. That is definitely not good news, man. Sure enough, it's this large angry mob with burning torches. They block the road and pelt the truck with stones and yell words I do not catch which, as you know, never fails to make things worse. A windshield cracks, the truck brakes and the men inside take cover.

It's toughened glass alright but those people outside look really mean and ready for just the kind of lone target we are. I am muddy and bruised and this day just seems to go on and on. Time to bail. The other men slide out from the driver's door. The torches approach. I sling my pack, kick the other door off and jump.

TWELVE

I jump into a semi-circle of angry faces in the light of the torches. A lot of hot words are being directed against the truckers. One of the outraged citizens carries a revolver. This seems to have become more and more common in Manipur in the recent past.

I really, really detest mobs. You can deal, in a tight spot, with professionals, armed to the pre-molars though they might be. You know where you stand and they know where they do. Each party just doing its job, each concerned with making sure things do not escalate. But with a mob like this, you never know what might happen. I mean, they really do not care if they hurt someone bad because by this time they are pumped up and not thinking on their own, it's like one of those collective thought things going on right there. That's why riots throw up the worst of violent excesses from otherwise normal people you can find. I discover later that the o.c. with the r. has warned the truckers that they would burn the vehicle for violating their precious blockade and that would be that. The boys are asked a lot of questions about what the truck contains–light machine parts and footwear–where they come from, who owns it and so on. The o.c.s leave in a bit, after posting a group to guard us, and the truckers scratch their heads. Immolation looks certain, as does a copious amount of bodily harm.

O.c. with the r. returns with a few young chaps after

some time and tells us something. The boys appear to protest and some sort of negotiation goes on. The o.c., in fact, is a representative of the Senapati District Students' Association (SDSA) which is masterminding the blockade, and he asks my transporters for Rs 5,000 to let the truck go. This, he tells them, is for the permit card his organisation gives to 'willing' and 'law-abiding' truckers. The boys pool their resources and come up with Rs 2,000 which they give at the local SDSA office where we are frog-marched to. In exchange they are handed a permit card. It says everything about the truck: its point of origin and destination, its registration number, and who has given the permit after 'necessary checks'. What it does not mention is what went into getting it. That is how a students' organisation has the power to decide which vehicles will be allowed to pass, and they even issue documents under their letterheads. They are the administration here.

I get a photograph of this 'permit' right down immediately afterwards, man. It says the whole story in black-and-white. Got the picture right here. Incid., the citizens don't bother too much with me. Actually they ignore me entirely which is fine by me because I get a ringside view to the whole thing. If only they knew I had a camera.

Manipur is only the latest state in the North-east whose students have begun harnessing their energies for 'productive' work like this. Assam showed the way to the others, a while earlier.

Back about thirty years ago, Assam's students launched an agitation against illegal migrant Bangladeshis. While immigrants had been increasing in the state for a long time before then, it was the students' energy which made the protests a mass movement and got practically everyone involved, and it was a good thing too. Those young people who marched on the roads and got a bit of the old stick treatment from the cops and were arrested and such, they were really idealistic and dedicated. Some, in token activities to shame the Assamese, took up menial work like cutting hair and pedalling rickshaws, these being the kind of jobs Assamese left for Bangladeshis to do.

Nothing much came out of that movement because the then PM got a deal with them and the Centre made a lot of promises. Illegal migration is an even worse problem, a crisis for the people, now than it ever was before. So, you'll ask, why isn't there another movement today?

That's 'cause of what happened to those original student leaders.

They became so popular they floated a political party whose name you might have heard of, and decided to stand for elections. Elder and wiser Assamese leaders advised them to let senior and distinguished Assamese stand for elections and guide the youth, but the students said no thank you, we're going to change things on our own. Good sentiment, but it doesn't work in the real world. Because as soon as they came to power with a landslide majority, they got to taste the real nature of political control. They were young, man, the chief minister and home minister were, like, twenty-seven or twenty-eight years old, and they were running a state that size.

That kind of power, it turned their heads. They also eventually realised that the Bangladeshis, who get into the electoral rolls and never miss voting, were this massive vote-bank everyone needed to stay in power, so they were cosying up to the same people they set out to remove from the homeland. Two terms at the helm, a lot of corruption charges, secret killings of ULFA leaders' families across the Valley, all kinds of shady deals and such later, they've lost the faith of the people. So if another generation of student leaders tries to fix social problems, the public doesn't get very enthusiastic, naturally. We've been bitten before.

But student unionism never went out of fashion and a lot of young people spend a lot of time doing student politics in colleges and universities, a kind of grooming ground for an eventual political career, same as in the rest of the country.

Assam's experiment at student politics is one empirical reason why I am not much for unions and such. Sure, young people have a lot of good ideas for fixing society. Sure, some of them might even be honest, and a lot of them, given a chance, might be hard-working and committed and so on. But actually administering a people, it's a big job, and it can turn anyone's head. I don't see why hard-working ordinary people should pay their taxes to subsidise education just so these young people can spend their time playing king-of-the-hill in a country where higher education is best made available for those who really deserve to study and do some good afterwards, as productive members of society.

So, anyway, the Assam experiment got every other student in the North-east going, and now you have all kinds of student organisations heavily into local politics. They mobilise at a snap of some idiot's fingers, have no problems with destroying public property and a bit of arson on the streets from time to time, and in Manipur, are deeply close to insurgent groups, just like all the other citizens' groups and such you have in that state. These blockades and things are a good way for them to earn money and by now they have become such a major force that political parties, local cops and the administration play along and never say a word.

We proceed from this middle-of-the-real-nowhere down the road as the valleys widen. It is night, there are barely any lights on in the few villages we pass, and the group is majorly subdued after all this. So after crossing a line of low hills, on the last stretch before Imphal, they just have to stop at a shady little joint where they can pump themselves up on a bit of spirit.

It is a small restaurant kind of thing and two other trucks are already there. From the way they mix their drinks under a lantern and drink quietly and urgently, my guess is they haven't paid liquor tax or whatever it is to local groups and militants, but they are determined to get a little tipsy before going on. They offer me a bit, they're really nice people, but seeing as I am not much interested they continue with a game of cards for a bit. Then we're on the road again.

Imphal is a huge plain circled by rolling hills, where most of Manipur's population is concentrated, like I said. They say it used to be a lake before. Dunno where the water went. Maybe there was an economic blockade of fresh water inflows and the lake upped and left, with no forwarding address. And why not? People do that.

I reach Imphal at nine in the evening. It has taken me more than sixteen hours for this minor distance from Kohima. The place is locked down, barricades on every arterial road coming into town, and cops are out on the streets, but Damu, one of the boys on the truck, and his brother who joins us at his house in Imphal insist they will help me fix an auto to a hotel and tell the auto chap to make sure I get a room for the night and that I do not go off wandering somewhere unsupervised *and* also warn him to charge a reasonable fare from me. Those guys were really good people. They never asked me unnecessary questions or bugged me, they always had a smile on the road and shrugged off the hardships on this stretch; they got along. They are a nice contrast to the town I land in. Imphal is more unfriendly than I remember it being before. Can't blame them, there are a lot of strange events happening. The hotel I stay in is much better than the one in Kohima, but that's because I had to take the first place I could find. Besides, a shady hotel in an already sticky town might not be a good idea. So this place, it has a TV in the lobby, while my room was painted a decent shade of cream back when the building was constructed, although the wall nearest the plank bed has got the usual alphabet plus alphabet message someone's left behind. They do have some decent furniture and room service, mainly heavily spicy fish, so that's okay. The first problem in this town is, however, language.

On no account, if you know Nagamese, must you speak it here. They don't like Nagas much these days, because the Naga rebels' map of a greater Naga homeland covers much of northern Manipur, where Tangkhul Nagas live. Not that the Manipuris are going to give up their land, but it figures they are not big fans of Nagamese anymore, if they had been earlier, which I somehow doubt. Manipuris don't know much Assamese, what with geographical distance and not having as much contact with the valley as the Nagas did back in the day, and they wouldn't like it either, being similar to Nagamese. Hindi, meanwhile, is not really welcome unless you want to stamp it on them that you're a total outsider, which for some of them means babe in the woods. Unfortunately, the hotel people don't know English either so I stick to Hindi and hope for the best, though they are mostly surly and pretend to be dense which I know they're not.

Imphal is like any other plains town elsewhere, discounting the hills in the distance. It has the appearance, as my friend N., who used to visit regularly for work and such from Guwahati, later put it, of being a town which had things going really smooth a while ago but has since fallen on bad times. This is totally accurate. Wide roads, decent-sized buildings, traffic, people on their way somewhere or the other, plenty of activity, but everything has a film of dust or disuse over it, like the machinery has stopped or is going to any moment, for no particular reason you can see at first glance. You get a feeling that the reason is very important, you even feel compelled to find out, but there is something in the air which convinces you, even before you start to examine things, that the answers might be dark and best left unexplored. When you understand the place in a while, you will realise that this initial instinct was not wrong.

Imphal valley, when I reach it, is in an uproar. What has happened is, in Thoubal district, just south of Imphal, a group of villages got tired of insurgents or UGs as they are called here (Underground Groups). So they asked the government the obvious question: UGs have guns, the Army has guns, paramilitary people have guns, cops have guns. Ergo, we want guns too, because no one is doing much good for us at the moment.

The government, for some reason, said yes and is in the process of giving them Lee-Enfields. Good rifles, but of doubtful effectiveness against assault rifles, even bad copies of good ones. The villagers are being trained into militia bands and the rule is they can only carry the guns in and around their villages, the government says.

Opinion is divided on this. Ordinary people feel this might lead to more violence if the newly-armed villagers start getting ideas, and this will not be a good precedent in the most disturbed state in the North-east. In the usually raging public space in this state, though, these ordinary voices are almost never heard. More political citizens' groups, like the Apunba Lup, protest, calling it failure of governance. You might think that's a good enough argument, but while in Manipur, you've got to understand the background to any political statement to see exactly what that statement means. The Apunba Lup has always been overtly pro-UG. I mean, they're the first to protest whenever a UG gets it in an encounter, but they are suspiciously low-profile when UGs kill ordinary people. When they choose to be, though, the Apunba Lup is so theatrically vocal, you have to watch them at work on the media. That kind of equation.

Speaking of the media, it works in mysterious ways in Manipur. Once again, there are ins, outs and what-have-yous at work everywhere. Local press outfits have sharply defined agendas and methods of operation, loyalties to work on, targets to focus and, in so many cases, rackets to run. They tread a fine line between running on the wrong side of the Constitution and making their friends on different sides happy. Who said this kind of journalism was easy?

Television channels have similar rules. Like in Guwahati, you've got to ask who owns the channel before you go on to analysing its coverage. This is true anywhere in the world, but much sharper, more naked in Manipur. And everyone familiar with how things work in this place, including the administration, central bureaucrats posted here, neutral folk, everyone knows this is the way things are run, so they work with or around this mechanism. On the TV, which I watch after a long time in the hotel lobby, the first news item is student leader Sapuncha Kangleipal fire-and-brimstoning against the government's 'desertion of its responsibilities', re the new village militia. He looks really pissed and is threatening all sorts of things including, surprise surprise, an agitation. Again, nothing extraordinary, from what I gather, that he does not mention why the villagers asked for weapons in the first place. Blinkered opinions abound. The second news item is the arrest of Kangleipal shortly after the press conference at the Imphal Press Club, cops marching in and dragging him off. This is news in the process of leading to further developments, because you can bet that everyone who is anyone will jump into the debate. I have other things to do, meanwhile.

I visit Kangla Fort, which, if you're in town, you must not miss even if you don't go anywhere else. Sure it's infamous now, after the strip protest by Meira Paibi (women's group) in front of its gates after the alleged rape and murder of Manorama Devi, a former militant. Back in 2004, after the protests, the fort was handed over to the government by the Assam Rifles.

The fort dates back to the seventeenth century, covers a wide area and is surrounded by a clear-water moat where you can see kayakers practise at dawn. Incidentally, Manipuris are seriously into different sports, as we all know, and they're very good, too. At dawn across Imphal you can meet joggers and marathon-runners every day. They are a very disciplined people.

The fort's walls are gone and only the base of the ramparts remains. Was a time the fort was on both sides of the Imphal river, but now it's only on one side so the river looks like it was meant to be a moat. Originally, though, it was a water source.

Kangla Fort is the heart of Manipur and the Manipuri people.

A word about the people, before we check the fort. See, back about AD 33 or thereabouts, there were seven clans of different people in this area, and you bet they used to fight among each other and so on. So this one guy, King Pakhangba, of one of the clans, he got all the elders of all the clans together at some place on the Imphal river, and led them across the river. On the other side he told them that now they were one people, the Meitei people. That's how they were tribes no longer and the rest of their history became much different from, say, the Nagas and Mizos nextdoor.

This is their history as I've heard it, as well as a lot of interesting comments from various people who are supposed to think a lot about such matters. This business about AD 33 is a bit curious, because this is very far back in time and who knows for sure, really, unless there are inscriptions and such which I haven't seen. But I suppose they came upon this figure, based on something or the other. Some guys I heard say it is curious that this year should be the same as when Jesus was crucified, and the river crossing sounds similar to John the Baptist and all that so maybe the dating could be connected to the coming of missionaries but I don't much consider this part because many things can happen in the same year around the world. Besides, this date is mentioned in one of their ancient chronicles, so I guess these theories are just the work of some people who think way too much and see connections where none exist.

Ed.: Try a simpler way of explaining how you think.

Whenever this river crossing might have taken place, it was *the* major moment for Manipur, because now the Meitei became a kingdom and remained so till the end of the nineteenth cent. A while after, they got Hinduism, but by then Pakhangba had become a god himself.

It is said that Kangla Fort was built by him, too, so it has always been associated with Meitei pride and such. Beginning with what must have been earthen fortifications, it became a bigtime citadel in the early seventeenth cent, after the then Manipuri king fought a war against a western Chinese kingdom called something or the other (Chinese history experts, please take a look and tell us, okay?). After he beat down the Chinese invasion force, he got a lot of captured soldiers and workers to build baked brick structures inside the fort, strengthened the walls and made it a grand complex spread over many acres. Very impressive it must have been, too.

Manipur was among the last places in the North-east to come under the Brits, along with Tripura. A bit before the Brits came in, Manipur went through its version of *Maanor Din*. Like 'The Days of The Maan' in Assam, Manipur had to face one furious invasion after the other by the Burmese kingdom of Ava. In Manipur's history, they call these dark days *Chahi Taret Khuntakpa*, which, if I understand correctly means 'The Destruction That Lasted Seven Years', so once again you get an idea of how bad it must have been back then.

Weakened and on its knees, the Manipur kingdom made a deal with the Brits and managed to have a subsidiary kind of alliance for the time being, with a Brit representative installed at the fort. But in the early 1890s, like they did elsewhere, the Brits tried to interfere or something in the succession, trying to get their candidate in place of some other guy.

This other guy, the genuine crown prince Tikendrajit, however, was not the sort to sit around, and he had had it up to here with Brit orders. So he got together a bunch of pissed-off soldiers and rebelled. I think the Brit representative got killed or something, troops were called in, the fort was besieged, there was some heavy fighting, the Brits bombed the fort's walls to small pieces, caught Tikendrajit and his military commander, and hanged them. The Brits abolished the kingdom (they were prolly looking for an excuse to do so) in 1893 or thereabouts, and that was that.

But today, Tikendrajit or its shorter version, Tiken, is a very common name among Manipuris. He was a hero.

Like the Sikhs, Meitei men took the surname of 'Singh', a custom which has continued today, as some of you doubtless know. There are other surnames common to general Hindu castes which also got exported here along with Hinduism.

As far as 'Singh' is concerned, there is a certain rule to the nomenclature which is, as I see it, universally observed here. At the beginning is the caste or clan name, then the name and then the lion reference. For instance, Thanaoujam Khogen Singh. The caste name is sometimes shortened: in this case to Th.

Dunno if the lion reference was effective for Meitei men, but in the early nineteenth century, during the Burmese invasions, the king was facing a shortage of fighting men (not surprising: the casualties must have been bad). So the king called for Muslim mercenaries from Bengal and elsewhere to add to his numbers, and their descendants constitute the Muslims of Manipur today. Mind you, I will have to check this story: I was only told this by Saidul, the Muslim driver of the van which took me southward from Imphal afterwards.

Inside Kangla Fort is an old decrepit palace which is being repaired by the government, a temple, things like that. The grounds are vast and on the lines of Burmese palace grounds. All these places actually bear resemblances to the Forbidden City. I suppose there's a template somewhere.

Kangla Fort, therefore, with all that history, is very important to Manipuris. There's a well somewhere which is said to have the soul of Pakhangba, lord of the universe, the same guy who united them back then. I haven't seen the well on my visits, but it must be somewhere, though why the lord of the universe would choose to live in a well is beyond me, if I may say so. That there well is the navel of the world, it is said, so maybe that's why he lives in it.

Inside the fort and in front of one of the palace-cum-temple complexes you'll see stone dragons built by the same captured Chinese workers I mentioned, but these were destroyed by the Brits. They are being reconstructed now.

Here's something interesting I found, meanwhile. Today, almost fully reconstructed, these dragons are white and three in number. Between us, they don't look much like dragons but who can say what a dragon is supposed to look like, eh? I mean, if you were to ever come across a dragon, would you tell him: 'Sir, excuse me, but you do not look like a dragon'? Thought so.

So, anyway, there are these three white dragons there today. But I saw some archival photographs, you know, taken by some Brit after the Tikendrajit rebellion when the fort was in the process of being gutted. That old pic shows two dragons. So, either the Brits, for some reason too convoluted for me to understand, blew up a dragon, got one of their guys to take a pic of the remaining two, just so they could reach beyond the grave, and cunningly knowing some government in the future would do some restoring, left the pics to confuse people like me. Or, option two: the government is trying to overcompensate for the arson back then and putting up three dragons just for the heck of it. I really don't know which is which.

The kings of Manipur were majorly into art and culture. Contemporary Manipuris have kept at it and produced some fine works of dance, theatre and such. Behind a large temple inside the fort is an open-air theatre where plays used to be performed. Facing the theatre arena, which is also being renovated, is a temple a few hundred years old, very impressive, in brick and stone, a bit crumbly, but they're fixing it so perhaps by the time you visit, it will look spruce.

There is a lot of area to cover inside the fort, obviously, and because so few people visit from outside Manipur, you'll not find much signage and such. Catching hold of these two local bureaucrat-type dudes, I ask them for general directions to reconfirm what I remember, which they give readily, but with the usual arched eyebrow-routine when I tell them where I am from. But, perhaps being more polite than the usual crowd, they do not give me further guidance on how to behave while in the state.

The main gate to the fort was a gabled structure with sloping delta roofs and very impressive, from photographs I have seen. The Brits took out this one too, they made a thorough job of the destruction. Afterwards, the government put up a replica, prolly of the same size or maybe a mite smaller, but, trust me, it doesn't look like anything except a pale copy of the original.

The rest of the town can be walked through and taken a look at, if certain things are kept in mind. More than most other towns in the region, while in Imphal it is essential to keep an extremely low profile and not stick out needlessly. Smoking in public is banned by the UGs, as is chewing paan masala and such, so if at all you need to smoke, do it on the q.t. I keep hearing stories of this or the other dude, if not a consumer a supplier or something, getting his hands chopped off for trading in the stuff, and at least some of the stories must be true. I mean, ever since Manipur got into the militancy routine in a big way in the early 1990s, it seems these groups have left nothing undone to make up for all the years Manipur had been quiet while Nagaland, Assam or Mizoram had so much conflict. So while these states are peaceful (or in the case of Assam, much more peaceful than before) all kinds of excesses keep taking place here. But if you mix in and just observe and not get noticed too much, it is okay for a visitor.

Imphal is also noted for having only two ATM machines. One of them is perpetually shut. The first time I saw it was shut I thought, okay, some glitch, maybe. But I have never seen it open over the years I have visited. Most mysterious. One imagines some top-secret covert op or experiment going on behind that SBI ATM shutter, man, the way they keep it locked. Why'd they put it up in the first place, anyway?

The other ATM, just across the road and up a side-road from the Kangla Fort gate, plays host to the Great Imphal ATM Trick, which is that town's sport. Unlike, say, Guwahati's sport, you require proper mass participation in this one. For the game to be played in its right spirit, you need approximately seven hundred Imphalites. For instance, say you are an Imphalite and so are half-a-dozen of your friends. Say you meet them for tea or something. After the usual round of greetings (in which you say *Dngai Lbra* which combines 'good morning/ afternoon/evening' with 'how are you?') one of your friends reveals that he might go to the ATM today. At this all of the gathering rejoice and bring out their ATM cards and hand them over to the volunteer. He victualises appropriately, says his prayers and goes and stands seven hundredth in line–or, if he is lucky, six hundred and ninety-ninth. Sometime this week he reaches the machine. You know what they say at ATM doors, that thing about only one person inside at a time or something? Forget it. The room is packed full of people and for added excitement SBI or the government or whoever is in charge of the place has dug this huge ditch outside it, filled the ditch with muddy water and placed a narrow wooden plank across on which another dozen citizens balance. The friend brings out one card, withdraws money. Then he brings out another card, ditto. Sooner or later someone mixes up the pin and everything goes blooey. And since everyone carries many cards it takes a long time to get your work done. It is an entertaining and educating sight. Since I do not carry much cash during hops I too get to participate in the festivities.

Pork and beef are not common unless you go to the Naga enclaves here. I settle mostly for fish unless I am up to visiting these enclaves. The Manipuri version of fish curry is passable but to this they add a side-dish of fish chunks in thick soup which is needlessly smelly and puts me off.

You will find many Manipuris in *dhoti* and a white sleeveless vest kind of thing. It is similar to the Parsi undershirt. Some men and women can be seen with–I guess–sandalwood paste on their foreheads. Hindusim took some time in settling among the Meitei, but when it did they took to it very strongly. By the early eighteenth, a king made Vaishnavism the state religion, so Manipuris today worship Krishna very seriously. But they have kept up an interesting connect to their indigenous beliefs. In most Meitei homes today you will find a shrine to Krishna and, beside it, another shrine to Pakhangba.

Once in this town, regardless of how long you're going to be here, you must visit the Ima Keithel. This translates into 'Mothers' Market', and that is exactly what it is. All the sellers, the helpers, the administrators are women and they run a very tight, efficient shop in a place which is fast running out of both qualities. They do great business, these thousands of hard-working Manipuri women. I have never seen anything similar anywhere, although in Shillong there are large areas of shops run by women, following from their social structure, and since women across the North-east don't wait around for equality and are not discriminated against at home, there are many shopkeepers and small traders everywhere. But here in Imphal, it is an exclusive zone. Also, if you are into the buying local clothes thing, this is the place to get the best bargains.

From Imphal, there are two ways to proceed forward through Thoubal district in southern Manipur. One is to Moreh due roughly southeast, where I am headed. The other, National Highway 150, is due almost dead south through the southern plains and then up the hills into the dinky town of Seling in Mizoram.

THIRTEEN

There are some words in some languages which can't be precisely translated into any other. That is, they can be, but what you might end up with is a collection of words which give only an approximation of the actual, original, meaning. Such words stand for concepts unique or uniquely expressible within that culture or value system. Therefore, you've got to know that culture, the people and all the unique elements comprising them to really understand what the concept means. This is a fascinating idea.

The Russians have a word like that: they call it *zemlya*. Russ-speakers here will tell you the word can be translated as 'land' in some usages, such as Novaya Zemlya ('New Land') or 'earth'. But for a Russian, the word has a bigger, deeper meaning: it means the world and *everything* in it. Not exactly universe, not exactly the galaxy or such, not a mere total of all the rivers, lakes, fields, forests and mountains you can find. Just the world. You have to be a Russian and to see the vastness of their land to understand both the necessity for such a concept and its significance. So you can translate *zemlya*, but not its actual meaning. And you might even understand zemlya, but you got to start *thinking* like a Russian to get it, really.

Here is another such word coming at you. Catch.

Tlawmngaihna.

Got it? I'll let you roll it around your tongues for a bit here till you get used to it. Takes some. I'd heard this word a few times before, but the exact meaning was explained to me very patiently by a chap while we were sitting on a grassy overhang near a ravine near a cute little village in Lawngtlai, deep in southern Mizoram near Myanmar, a while back. The concept was so amazingly simple that it took me a while to understand why it took a deal of explaining in any other language. But you have to really understand what the word means, to comprehend the single unified concept at the base of the lives of Mizos.

Tlawmngaihna is many things (don't groan like that, I'm trying my best to be incisive here). It is what you might call an obligation on every Mizo, a sort of requirement which has absolutely no room for *not* carrying it out. This obligation involves, in equal parts, kindness and hospitality to other people, assistance of whatever sort and a deal of other nice things which could be in any wishful notice for better civic behaviour in any part of the world. What really sets this concept apart is the degree of self-effacement involved.

That is, you've got to be kind and humble at the same time and not even be consciously telling yourself that you are following an obligation. This, if I get it right, turns the idea right around into a very powerful moral force. And that word up there means all of this, get it? I'm still not sure if I explained this clearly enough, but if you ever meet a real authentic Mizo you'd get my point.

But before all that, a little note. 'Mizoram' means land of the Mizos, as you might have guessed. It does not make the news much these days, but still, whenever an anchor or a likewise congenitally clueless being pronounces it '-ram' like the Hindu god, it makes people back there wince. It is not '-ram' like the Hindu god or '-ram' like 'the truck rammed into the clueless news anchor'. The 'a' is very, very short. Just try to pronounce it as short as possible and you pass. That's better, yes.

Mizoram marks a certain departure from the norm in the North-east in that there is a clear majority of one people here. We'll not go into theories about where they came from because that, like everywhere else in the North-east, will make you go cross-eyed.

There are, then, mostly one people here, and back in the time of the Brits they were called Lushai and the state as we know it today was called the Lushai Hills District. I will further mortify you here by translating that 'Lushai' means 'people who play with heads'. Nudge-nudge, wink-wink and you can draw your conclusions from there, I'm not prompting you.

However, the Brits, as was their custom, got the nomenclature out of whack because the Lushais were not the only people in the Lushai Hills. There were a bunch of others, the big ones being Hmar, Ralte and Paite. All these tribes, put together, are called Mizo which generally means 'People of the Hills' and I have, I think, explained things very clearly and what's the word . . . eruditely, yes, here, so please do not get confused. There are some other small tribes as well, two of which have their own autonomous districts within Mizoram.

Today Mizoram is among the most peaceful states in the North-east. Not a trace of an insurgent lurking in the undergrowth, if you look around. Which could be one reason it does not figure much on TV because, as we all know, national news channels *love* reporting on insurgents from the region. Any other news would be s-o-o boring, na?

Things were not always so, and it wasn't about ethnic identity, unresolved geography or modern administration clashing with ancient systems but about . . . rats. Yep, rodents. Here's the story.

Mizoram, like the rest of the region, has a lot of bamboo forests, and very beautiful they are to look at, too, besides being useful, traditionally, for building all kinds of household products and cheap construction material. But once in a while, bamboo trees flower, you know. Now I can see some hands raised back there and I know you'll say 'but bamboo is a type of grass' and all that trivia which is true but take my word for it, they flower, and that is what is important for this story, so let me continue.

In Mizoram, when large patches of bamboo forest suddenly flower, rats start eating them, greedy pests that they are. This, in turn, leads to happy rats, which leads to many happy baby rats and they have to feed even more. Soon enough, the bamboo forests are not enough for them so they invade the homes of the luckless Mizos and raid their rice stores. Ergo, no rice, plus rat-borne disease.

This has been happening for a while now, but back in the late Fifties, it was really terrible. So a bunch of Mizos got together and asked the government to do something about it, but with not much happening in the line of relief and medicine, they armed themselves, formed a group called the Mizo National Front and sort of quit the Union.

There followed a running battle between the Union and the MNF through the Sixties, with the public solidly behind them and the guerillas performing rather well on home ground. In 1966, Aizawl became the first and, I believe, the only urban area in India to be bombed by the Indian Air Force which kind of goes to show how serious the fighting must have been.

Six years later, the Centre made Mizoram a Union Territory and, in '87, a state. The MNF won the elections. All of which has still not solved the problem of the rats to everybody's satisfaction because famine returns each time the bamboo forests flower.

So today when I see people down south and elsewhere demanding statehood I think 'at least Hyderabad (or anywhere else) is not being bombed by the IAF'.

As an aside: the Mizos have done with their fighting and settled down which is why there isn't any insurgency there anymore. It, along with Arunachal and Nagaland, is today the most peaceful part of the North-east and just as safe, or perhaps safer, than your city. Meghalaya comes in after them, Assam somewhat behind because of a few isolated incidents, but with hopes of catching up quickly. Tripura has some distance to go, dunno when it will and Manipur, well, you know. Those are the ratings, right there.

The road up from Manipur gets much better in the hills and Mizos are kind of serious about infrastructure, particularly transport, as they should be, they fought a lot for statehood so it is a matter of pride for them to keep the place properly. Some parts of the road occasionally give way to mud tracks but it is not as uncomfortable as it might appear.

On foot, though, it is a different matter. Mizoram is not walking country. The hills are far too steep and angular, the hill roads too inclined and hairpin, but sometimes you get spectacular views and occasionally a level stretch, but you got to watch out for zippy cars. If you are familiar with the place you can take side tracks and if you get lost you can ask for directions, no problem, people will guide you around. The absence, on the whole, of walking areas is compensated by picturesque villages where I have usually found someone or the other to spin a story and make roast beef the right way, sometimes simultaneously, which is saying something.

The general altitude is a thousand metres and up, but it does not rain here as much as in Meghalaya or Arunachal.

But a walker's loss is an angler's feast. There is simply an abundance of rivers and streams here with all kinds of fish, if you have the patience, because hill fish are very clever. If you find yourself in Lawngtlai in southern Mizoram, make it a point to check the Kaladan river (it has another name but this is easier to remember). The view is spectacular, the fish plenty, and the breeze constant. The Kaladan flows in from Myanmar and goes back there, and like other rivers in Mizoram, used to be an easy way to travel to Myanmar, or Chittagong in what is Bangladesh today. Independence put an end to all that but each time I visit I hear some project or the other to revive these waterways. Lessee.

Any botanists in the crowd? I think I spotted someone when I was talking about Arunachal. Perhaps you've been there, ma'am. Mizoram has a huge variety in plants, particularly medicinal herbs and such. The tribes in the old days figured all this out, but for me they are just pretty flowers and green shrubs. But they are an important part of Mizoram's ecology and I hope you'll take a look for yourself.

There are a whole bunch of lakes too, if you are a lake person, but if someone tells you to visit the Rih Lake he is making a double joke. For one, Rih is on the other side of the Myanmar border, although all that was historically Mizo land. For another, in pre-Christian times, souls had to pass through Rih to reach Mizo heaven. I have heard that Rih is beautiful but, between us, I believe I'll wait a while before finding out for myself.

Mizos are a shade or two different from, say, Baptist Nagaland or Catholic Goa.

The Presbyterian Church is the predominant force in almost all parts of Mizo life, and almost solely responsible for such nice things as the phenomenally high literacy rate, at nearly 90 per cent the second highest in India. But it also comes down hard on a few things in ways which would make the shrillest hellfire-and-damnation Baptist preacher seem like a dissolute rocker.

Take the matter of alcohol, for e.g. The P.C. woke up one morning and summarily banned the stuff through the state and has not relaxed it since. This single pronouncement sent bootleggers rapturous with joy, I am told, and tipplers with cultivated tastes into perpetual mourning. Much like Gujarat, Mizoram today has a parallel bootleg economy and one unexpected offshoot has been that the local stuff, *zu*, seems to get better all the while, provided you know where to look for it and whom to ask.

Aizawl is right up there in the contest for the most scenic hill town in India. Where it scores the most is it is much cleaner than a lot of its close competitors. Water, as I've said, is scarce in the hills, but there is not much dust in Aizawl to clean off and Mizos are a scrupulously neat people and will remind you, if you stay at a hotel there, to be likewise. At which point you remember tlawmngaihna and cooperate with them because, after all, who wouldn't, with such nice hosts? Tlawmngaihna might be an old tribal concept but the early Presbyterians made a neat transition of it and besides, if I have my New Testament correct, Jesus talked a lot along similar lines.

An additional highlight, as you walk up and down Aizawl roads and remember to greet shopkeepers, particularly on Sundays, is this: there might not be another town in India where a street direction would include 'Walk down Zion Street'. It sounds, particularly the first time you hear it, like a blessing of great power. Walk down Zion Street. Neat.

And then you notice shop names and house names: Moses Tailors, Bethlehem Villa, Israel Confectioners. This is not merely Christianity, you see. There are a lot of Jews here. They are the Bnei Menashe. For a long time, they practised Judaism by themselves, but in recent years, I've been told, converted formally to Judaism. Dunno about the exact rules which allow people to convert to Jewism but, you see, the Menashe claim to be among the famous lost tribes of Israel, although they don't look Jewish.

Hmm. I just made a statement there I must qualify. There are Jews and there are Jews. If you've met a Jew originally from Israel, you've seen a certain type. Then there are European Jews who might or might not look like typical Jews. Then there are Ethiopian Jews who look like other Ethiopians but that is alright because everyone through history has known about the Jews of Ethiopia, so if an Ethiopian named Solomon Abraham lands up in

Haifa with a birth certificate he gets citizenship like *that*. However, chances of this happening are not much because back in the Seventies, Israel airlifted most of the Ethiopian Jews straight out of that country during some civil war or the other.

In India, in parts like Thane and elsewhere, there are Bnei Israeli Jews, descended from those who had landed in India centuries earlier. Their provenance is not doubted, nor is the fact that they preserved their traditions very well.

The Bnei Menashe, who look like other Mizos, are a different bird, so to speak, and their story is kind of complicated. It begins in the 1950s with a Mizo getting a dream in which he, if I remember the story right, was told by someone or the other that the ancestor of the Mizos was the same guy mentioned in the Old Testament and other Jewish texts as the leader of one of the tribes which were taken away from Israel a long time ago and sort of vanished from history, making them one of the lost tribes, Israel's version of the Holy Grail. So what this guy does, he gets a few followers and sets off from south Mizoram for Israel on foot. This idea is so awesome by itself that I must pause for a moment here and applaud his lunacy. It is right up there with the best of them.

After a bit, seeing as it would be a long hike, they turned back and what they did not achieve by reaching Israel they attempted at home, namely spreading what they said was the original word of Yahweh and urging their fellowmen to turn their backs on Christianity. Thirty years or so on, this group reached out to organisations in Israel which trace Jews and bring them back to the Holy Land. Nearly a thousand Bnei Menashe left for Israel, but not on foot this time.

This began a serious of events increasingly weird in character. Conservative Jews, on seeing the Menashe landing in Judea and immediately being sent to colonise Jewish settlements in what are known in the Arab world as the Occupied Territories, questioned whether these Jews were indeed authentic or just a bunch of people trying to take advantage of Israel's policy and thus migrating to a more developed country.

A committee came over to Mizoram and checked how the Menashe live here, and it was quite an investigation, because you see, between the old fellow's dream and the committee's arrival, the Menashe had become as Jewish as anyone can be without turning into Charlton Heston lookalikes and going around hitting small, medium and large bodies of water with a staff and urging people to join the NRA. Alright, that was a little mixed-up, but the point is, the Menashe had been living as orthodox Jews and practising their religion with great diligence. Impressed, the chiefest chief rabbi in Israel declared they were indeed children of Abraham and called for their return.

You'd say that's a happy ending, but *non, m'sieur*, there be no happy endings in politics, only things getting murkier. For one, the chiefest chief rabbi in Jerusalem laid a condition that the Menashe formally and officially convert to Orthodox Judaism before leaving India. For another, the Mizo Presbyterian Synod had been getting increasingly antsy about the Menashe calling on Christians to return to Judaism, so Christian groups complained to the Indian government about these conversions, and what they termed one country (to wit, Israel) interfering in the internal demographics and stealing people from another country (to wit, us). So the Ind govt did some back-and-forth with the Israelis and the conversion/immigration stopped.

Meanwhile, feeling a little left out, perhaps, what with the Jews and Christians and two national governments in the mix and no one inviting them, Hindu groups began backing the Menashe, saying if the government did not come down hard on Christian missionaries converting people from other religions to their fold, why should the government get bothered if the Jews were converting a few Christians into theirs, eh?

This little political cluster ... um, *fest* (I have resolved not to use objectionable language here so I am trying very hard but it is quite an effort so you need to appreciate it, people) would have continued and conceivably involved yet more people and groups wholly unrelated to the issue but which invariably feature in badly-written conspiracy thrillers, including perhaps the Freemasons (who have a large presence in India), the Opus Dei (which has an *even larger* presence) and the Thackerays, who might have doubtless found a Mumbai connection, if the Israelis had not come up with an ingenious improvisation, as Jews usually do.

Um, was that racist? Did I just make a racist statement? The Cid is deeply contrite if he did, but the fact remains that the Israelis did indeed come up with a solution, suggesting that the Menashe should go to Nepal, convert to Orthodox Judaism there, and then go to Israel. Everyone happy. I have to check the exact situation today, though.

Ed.: There are very few people who can tell a story and piss everyone off in the process. Presenting one of them.

There are more than 10,000 Menashe in Mizoram and a tiny part of Thoubal district in Manipur. Interestingly, the Menashe are the single-largest community of Jewish settlers in the West Bank and the Gaza Strip, thus giving their relations in Mizoram cause for worry whenever there is violence in those parts, as there usually is.

The Menashe's claims that they have always practised Judaism since the time they reached Mizoram a few thousand years ago is sometimes disputed by scholars and learned people, who make a counter-claim that the people of Mizoram were all completely animist, like everyone else, till the missionaries first reached the hills, and this Judaism business is actually what is termed in theological circles as revivalism, or, if I get the concept right, a group laying claims to being an integral part of a religious tradition it has only recently joined.

I have absolutely no idea what is and isn't, but the Menashe's synagogues and prayer baths and such are impressive to visit, as is their utter devotion to Judaism impressive to witness.

Also, consider this interesting bit: y'see, the Menashe have (and this is a confirmed fact) got a song which they've been singing at harvests, along with other Mizos and Kukis, for ages. This song includes an FPA (which means, dawgs, First Person Account) about running away from enemies, crossing dry-shod over water, following a cloud of dust and a pillar of fire, and having the satisfaction of seeing their enemies drown when the aforementioned water closed in after them, as it would have, the nitwits. While any academic will tell you that religious beliefs around the world do have a lot of uncanny similarities, this one, which could be so much a re-telling of Exodus, is worth thinking about.

Whichever way you look at it, if you walk down Zion Street in Aizawl and want to get, say, a prayer cap from Moses Tailors, it will be a nice story to tell later, I say.

Sidelight two (and this one occurred to me independently, okay?) is the Mizos' eclectic taste in music. Apart from the as-good-as-Shillong choirs which you must listen to, and the usual rock bands you hear at music shops, Mizos also seem to be going in for a lot of rap, though not hardcore gangsta rap which might, one imagines, get the Presbyterian Synod to suffer multiple coronaries and burst arteries and such.

Speaking of music, I want to give you another bit of trivia you might want to keep in mind. The bamboo dance has become a synonym for Mizo dances, and the general idea seems to be that it is some sort of harvest ritual and a happy occasion. This is, sadly, not so. In pre-Christian Mizoram, the tribes used to have the Cheraw dance (that is what it is called) as a kind of memorial service for women who died in childbirth *which* is why, in case you have ever wondered, it is always danced by women. Which does not take away from the fact that it is a very difficult form to get a hang of, but if you listen to the songs which accompany them, you will realise that it is a very solemn affair.

Then there used to be a series of three festivals called *Kut*, based on the seasons and the harvest, roughly paralleling the three Bihus in Assam. These are relatively minor under the Church, but still around.

In case you have a Mizo friend who invites you over for

the evening and there is a small gathering which proceeds to get (illegally) drunk, there will be invariably a round of singing. This quaint social ritual is a derivation of old tribal gatherings, but one element which has remained even today is that you can make up the songs yourself, only making sure that they rhyme in three lines. Try it sometime: spin a tale of how awesome you are or something.

Mizoram, along with Tripura, has been historically the least connected with the Brahmaputra Valley. Their connections could be said to have extended till the Barak Valley in modern Assam. The rivers linked them more with Myanmar and with east Bangladesh. From Mizoram, it is a somewhat hairy journey down National Highway 40-A into Tripura through the western mountains, so a better idea would be to head north into south Assam and then into Tripura. I'm just trying to make your journey easier, thassall. You want to take the NH 40-A, fine by me, dude.

FOURTEEN

Tripura is the Exceptional State.

Before I go into that, a little business I need to get over with. I like the American custom of giving nicknames to their states. Sunshine State, Lone Star State, Garden State and such. These are whimsical and colourful terms of reference, whether or not the original nicknames have much relevance today. People from these states sometimes use these nicknames in everyday conversation, sometimes in self-deprecation. They are a part of the common lexicon. We should have something on similar lines here, something to celebrate geography, history or even a name in jest. I don't know if we actually do, or if there is a bunch of names in a dusty file somewhere that some serious learned fellow cooked up but which no one bothered to popularise afterwards. I'm not sure. Do we?

Perhaps this is because we take things too seriously when it comes to self-image, community, language and such, and run the risk of inflamed passions in case some state gets a funny name. Things are complicated enough as they are.

But if we did, Tripura would be the Exceptional State, because it is an exception to virtually every rule in the other six states of the region. It hasn't seen tribal republics in over two thousand years. Forget about hill state, it does not even have a hill district. It features the least amount of mist per square yard (a measure I have independently created for no scientific reason I can think of and has no use whatsoever but since I created it, it is an official standard). Historically, the people of Tripura had the least interaction with the other states and tribes, and more with Bengal. *And* it has monuments at par with the rest of the country.

Tripura is, of course, what the rest of the country calls it. Its people call it Twipra, a useful thing to know when you find yourself there and suspect that what the locals call it sounds a little different than expected.

This oddity, however, has got nothing to do with history. The local form of the name is derived from its official form, whose etymology could be based on any of three or four reasons which I shall leave to you to discover because I don't know them.

The main thing you have to remember is the Exceptional State is a bit of a different experience than the other states in the region. Historically, its people, its culture and language have been influenced by eastern Bengal. Its tribes were close to the people of the Chittagong Hill Tracts, that bit of north-south-lying corridor in eastern Bangladesh which is predominantly tribal and has, since 1971, been facing a lot of state persecution in that country. Naturally, we get to hear very little of these atrocities, but eastern Bangladesh has been a big influence, for good or evil, on Tripura's recent history.

Tripura is mostly plainland with a few rivers flowing through it. Very little of it is hilly, and the vegetation is like anywhere in Bengal or the Brahmaputra Valley. This is one of the reasons why Hinduism spread very quickly into it, and so did monarchy. Tripuri kings claimed direct descent for more than 2,000 years, protected as they were in the north and east by their hill state neighbours and in the south by the CHT. There *are* tribes in Tripura, but they have been more closely assimilated with other people than in any other state around.

All those hills around might have brought it some protection, but it also meant that Tripura never grew bigger than what you see today. But it is a crowded place, by gum. Though it is the third-smallest state in the country, its population is the second-highest in the North-east.

As with the fate of the rest of the region, Tripura's fate got mixed up with the events of the Raj. For some reason, the Brits did not bring fire and destruction into the tiny kingdom, and its transition into a princely state was real slick. Easy to administer with the local big guy still on his throne, that must have been the Brit policy, at least in this case.

This led to the Tripuri kings getting a lot of notions into their heads. First among them was a very European coat-of-arms, which has two lions rampant, a betel leaf, all kinds of bells and whistles, flags and a furled banner at the base.

The second idea they got was construction.

The kingdom had always gone in for royal architectural statements in a big way, influenced by monarchies in Bengal, but after British peace, the kings decided to let loose.

There used to be a royal palace about 10 km out of Agartala, a site I should have visited but haven't, sorry. In my defence I should say that there is not much to see there.

The same earthquake that knocked down Christ Church in Guwahati in 1897 called on this palace too, and utterly took it out. The king, doubtless roused out of his ancestral home in his slippers, was thus left without an appropriately magnificent showcase of his kingdom. He then decided, like a true despot, to build *another*, even bigger palace, this one in the middle of Agartala town as it is today.

Tripura at that time was in a deal of trouble, partly because of the earthquake and partly from a very bad economy. But the king appears to have spent not less than a million good ones on his new home, which caused a lot of muttering and pissed-off subjects and such, which he doubtless laughed away.

Ujjayanta Palace, notwithstanding the circumstances of its construction and its effect on the people of Tripura, is one of the biggest, possibly *the* biggest, monument of its period in the region. It is also certainly beautiful, designed by some old Brit with a lot of influences visible in it if you know how to look.

As palaces go, at two storeys it is not really very impressive, but definitely so for a small kingdom on the brink of famine and civilian unrest. Plus it is in white, which gets extra points in my book for sheer lunacy, because in a land with so much rainfall, the last colour you want on your walls is white, which has the effect of paper with rain stains on it in a few decades.

Ujjayanta Palace has got individually crafted rooms and such inside but today they've gone and made it the State legislative building so you might not get to see it in its entirety and they've made some modifications and things to it to suit sarkari needs, all of which is a let-down. You might also not be allowed to walk around its gardens which are like kilometres across in area and very pretty.

Some fellow told some other fellow who told me that the gardens were modelled after the Rashtrapati Bhawan but since I get to hear that about any Raj-era garden I visit, I'll pass on that one until independently verified.

There are other monuments worth a look. Second on the list is the Neer Mahal, a real authentic lake palace in the middle of the Rudrasagar Lake near this small village called Melaghar, a little more than 50 km from Tripura. It might appear a long trip on those roads, but it is definitely worth a look. It has, among other things, this big room which used to be a dancing hall, the king who built it in 1930 being inclined to such pursuits, and is actually very solidly constructed. There is this other room built, it seems, just for the king to play chess.

This king also seems to have had his priorities right because he got the palace built just so he could get on a boat and be ferried to his bedroom in an outer wing, where he could step off the boat into the room. That's a very neat idea.

Besides it being a lake palace and all, another reason for visiting the place is the lake itself and its surroundings are full of various migratory birds in winter, when it looks particularly picturesque. There are a few other palaces scattered around the state which should also make the list.

Agartala is a bit crowded, otherwise, but you can find good accommodations and the people are hospitable. If you know Bengali you can get along fabulously. They do not go in for experimental food like in the hills, but they make fish really nice and they don't have the stinky soup of Manipur, so you will eat twice the usual amount of fish you would have had just to be thankful.

There is this one place about 75 km from here over roads which might be repaired by the time you reach. Debotamura is on the banks of this river Gomati and is basically this big wall of a rocky mountain, into which are carved these massive images of Hindu gods. It is impressive to look at and is about four hundred years old and looks it. There are these two other places elsewhere with similar carvings too, but since I haven't seen them there's not much I can tell you, although I keep hearing they are just as impressive, so they must be.

The Tripureshwari Temple, which also goes by other names, is the most important place here for Hindus and also on the list of national Mother Goddess sites. It is at Udaipur town, also a bit more than 50 km southwest from Agartala. Udaipur, if you visit, has some other places of interest, including a batch of temples and some lakes which are surprisingly clean and kept well, when seen last.

If, on the other hand, Buddhism is more in your line, you can go to any one of, I think, more than half-a-dozen Buddhist temples. The nearest from Tripura is tiny Venuban Vihar, about 12 km away, and is usually a quiet place.

Now these idols they have at the temples, they're interesting. Practically every one of them, from what I gather, was brought in from Burma back then, and you can see that in their construction.

Considering the state is more than 60 per cent forest, at least on paper, there are just these two wildlife sanctuaries you might consider taking a look at: Trishna and Sipahijala. But you will get to see many varieties of orchids whether you go to these sanctuaries or not, and they are one flower you can't have enough of, no matter how much time you've just spent up in Arunachal. So that's a good thing.

Tripura got into a spot of bother back in 1971 when a large number of Hindu Bengali refugees fled there from East Pakistan. Conversely, a large number of Muslims from here left between 1947 and '71, so quite a part of the demographics got changed. This led to ethnic problems, as usually happens after large population displacements.

The tribal population of Tripura, following this, began to feel that they were being left out of the general scheme of things, and Hindu Bengali speakers were kind of taking over power. So, over the years, several tribal militant groups emerged and had vicious clashes with non-tribals. This continues even today although a few groups have entered into dialogue.

But it's not just these militants on their own, you see. The people they represent are also at each other once in a while, and some terrible riots have taken place. These matters are far from being fixed, as things stand today, so Tripura is grappling with some really complicated, deep-seated problems.

That could be true of the whole of the region. I mean, the complicated issues part. See, independence, democracy, progress and all are very good and have worked out well for the rest of the country, as they have to some measure here. But there are so many different people who live here next to one another, with so many convoluted relationships of different natures and degrees that resolving them takes some inspired leadership from those who govern, and some letting-go by the people. Neither has happened as much as one might wish. So these frictions continue. This comes from the way the land was settled and shaped over many hundreds of years, and was bound to happen some time or the other. These disturbances do not mean the land is accursed or the people are fundamentally wrong. People are just people, and they react to issues according to their lights. I mean, there are such ethnic or caste-based or religious issues elsewhere in the country too, and they do erupt sometimes. In the North-east there are just many shades of them, that's all.

Someday, all the other unresolved problems in the region will be sorted out and the people will go on with their lives. But, otherwise, the place is just like any other on earth, maybe a shade more beautiful, a shade more naturally unspoilt, a shade more complicated and therefore fascinating in trying to understand, and totally worth travelling in. From a distance, reading the land in a newspaper, you get all sorts of notions. Just don't trust everything the papers tell you: they don't give you the usual, the ordinary, the commonplace, the normal. I work in them. I know.

FIFTEEN

At Imphal, I wait for some traffic on the roads before coming out, just a precaution you know. There are still policemen and some paras at street corners, folding away the barricades from the night before. The town has been mostly peaceful except someone found an unexploded grenade near the legislative assembly two evenings earlier.

There are some buses south to Thoubal district and so on, but I am not even going to try for them. They are very few in number and chances are they might not run regularly. Best stick to small transport vehicles.

So I catch a van to Moreh in the far south-east, on the Myanmar border. Forty-six kilometres of this is through the plains of southern Imphal and Thoubal districts, the rest through the southern mountains. My co-passengers are a strange lot, because though it is much before noon, they want to stop at the last village before we climb into the hills. It is like they have developed a different bio-rhythm just for this route. Y'see, there are no restaurants in the hills, not before Moreh. The remaining 87 kilometres is through almost completely deserted country, so they have to stock up in that last village for the rest of the drive. I try to adjust to this logic as best as I can.

Never buy packed food at these last-village types. No one eats packed food, chocolates and all in these parts, so, nine times out of ten, such food will have expired. Check the bottled water in such places too, no matter which part of the country you are in. Or, if there are such multi-phase journeys on your road, best to carry your water from the last biggest town.

The roads from Imphal out are very badly potholed, and as far back as I have seen have never been fixed. The villages and towns we pass are full of moderate bustle and things appear safe. From about ten kilometres out of Imphal, at intervals of five kilometres or so stand groups of youths manning stop points, and you can bet some of them are armed. These barricades consist of bamboo posts attached to a pillar at one end and pulled at the other by rope, like cops have, one end weighted down with stones. These youths are neither militants nor Manipur police. They seem to be among the growing band of unemployed young men of semi-rural and rural Manipur who have found, in the state's fast-drying distance passenger and cargo transports, 'a convenient milch-cow with a cornucopian udder' as the man says.

You can't get around these checkposts, even if you wanted to, which the transport vans know better than to even try, because they have to return along these roads, you know. Rates and such are known by everyone and not a single vehicle gets away. If you tried, say sped through before they lowered a gate, they call ahead at another, which is lowered and waiting, and you have to pay more and get shouted at for dissing the men. No one, not the cops, not the army, not all the concerned citizens in this land who love speaking to the media and laying out plans for Manipur's salvation, no one ever tells them to remove the checkpoints.

You could say this is so unbelievable it's a wonder these

young men do it with such impunity. But in this state, such extra-constitutional practices are the rule. What would be unbelievable is if anyone remarked on it.

At a petrol pump 30-odd kilometres from Imphal, where we stretch our legs while the van gets tanked up, I see a curious, funny and sad sign. In large red letters, in Manipuri, it says: 'Please do not throw bombs inside the petrol pump.' And here you thought the odd careless cigarette was a petrol pump's worst enemy, didn't you? Not much rain has fallen in Imphal Valley, at least much less than normal, which accounts for some of the dust flying around. As we climb into the hills, the vegetation becomes scrubby and the trees dry. Occasionally we cross small homesteads built on wooden stilts, with the base for storing firewood for the winter or food for livestock. An emaciated cow is tethered to a tree nearby, and little piglets wallow in small pens. Man, even the pigs look thin. These homesteads lead a bare-bones existence, selling the pigs and what little crops their terrace-farms cultivate, at the nearest market. Life in these parts has never been better than what it is today, so it's not just a reflection of the state's economy as it stands today (which, of course, is on very shaky legs).

Cultivation here has always been a struggle with low productivity, less rain, unhelpful terrain and all the other factors a very pessimistic farmer would dread. Because the hills this side of the leeward do not catch much rain, irrigation and other necessities are hard to obtain, so subsistence farming has been the norm here. This time round, with the rest of the valley dry like that, this place nearly crackles, it is that parched.

You can, therefore, easily imagine the people who live in the southern hills: they reflect the land. Occasionally you see them go by the car window, thin, pinched faces, wiry legs, big loads of firewood on their backs, or buckets of water from some deep, nearly dry well, climbing up the terraces to their farms.

The road gets much worse as we continue southward and the van lurches from side to side. The passengers and their luggage are thrown about and my right side begins to throb again. Paramilitary and Manipur Reserve Battalion checks become more frequent the further up the hills we go. This part sees a lot more militant activity than the plains usually do, although, if you look at it from the UGs' points of view, striking at Imphal would be more prestigious and all.

The paras make all the males in the cars get off and walk through the checkposts while the cars are driven through to some distance ahead, where they wait while we walk up and get in. The paras check the cars sort of thoroughly to make sure none of us is carrying weapons and such, and only let us get inside the car at a very safe distance from their posts. While this might be a practical necessity to prevent drive-bys, it seems they do not consider that Manipuri UGs are equal-opportunity organisations, because they don't ask the women to get out for checks. I'm not saying they should, but if the whole logic behind these measures is more security, what's stopping some woman UG inside a car from firing, I say. It doesn't make sense, and besides they don't even have women cops on these roads to check passengers.

At the top of this southern mountain range you get to

see magnificent views, like real deep valleys far below. Even in the dry heat up there, in the middle of the day, there is always mist of varying density far away, or floating around in the cool valley floors below. Man, if we were allowed access and these places were safe, it would be such a beautiful country to explore, walking along some narrow stream under the trees in these ravines.

We descend on gentle ribbons from here south-eastward, but this does not make the drive any smoother, because the road is practically gone. There are like these huge sharp stones in the middle and the axles barely take the shock each time, as do our backs. It would have been much worse had it rained and the van got stuck in some thick deep mud. Along the descent you get to see border fences here and there, the same line reappearing around a hill. The fences here are about twenty feet tall and of thick steel, in quadrilateral shapes. I'm sure you've seen similar types elsewhere. They're not very impressive because they don't have more than a single roll of barbed wire on top, if you've seen fences along the Pakistan border and think that's the norm around the country. The truth is, India's international borders' impressiveness is related to the country across the border.

At least they've got fences here, at Myanmar. Along Lower Assam's river basins and marshes, or the southern foothills of Meghalaya, there is hardly any suggestion that on the other side is Bangladesh. Because the Meghalaya people are clear they don't want Bangladeshis up there with them, the government has built some fences, but in Lower Assam these fences are far from being completed. In some places, the BSF patrols the rivers and the government says it is virtually impossible to build fences here, but in other parts they could have, you know, if only there had been greater political will, if only whichever party is in power stopped being cosy with the migrants. But these matters will not change any time soon.

At Myanmar, then, you won't find thickly-barbed fences and mean, tall border guards: that type is meant to impress Pakistanis. A working fence was put up over the years, mainly because the Myanmar government, which has its own insurgencies to deal with, kind of convinced the Indian government to at least do something on this side.

One measure of the importance of an international border for the army that defends it is this: the next time you are at one of these places, check not just for barbed-wire but also for lights on top. Along the China border we have lights at regular intervals, though, between us, if the PLA comes marching over the mountains again it will take more than *lights* to stop them.

Here, in these parts, there are no lights. You will not remark much on this absence in the day, but think of this place on a moonless night, under the clouds. Think of a few bribed guards of the BSF, India's most corrupt paramilitary force bar none. Think of what a few cuts here and there can do. That's the border here.

We go past a hill, steep and exceptionally green. Beyond is an angular valley. I am going to climb this one, I tell myself. Some hills, they just send out these messages in big blinking letters: 'Climb Me.' This is one of those. We descend, at last, to Moreh, and beyond are the valleys of Myanmar.

SIXTEEN

Imagine a nearly circular ovoid. Place a chord (surely you remember what a chord is: a straight line drawn from one point on the circumference to the other, whose length is less than the diameter, in case of a circle) at one end, practically at the extreme. Place a point halfway down this chord. Now rub out a small part of the circumference on one side of the chord, and another part on the other end of the oval.

The chord is the India-Myanmar border. The very small area on one side is Indian territory. The point on the chord is the last Indian border town of Moreh. Beyond that is the Tamu area of Myanmar. The two erasures are two passes that lead into this plain. This should not be difficult to picturise.

It is fringed by difficult hills at either end. The road to Moreh passes through the western pass, which is guarded by the Assam Rifles. The arrangement, therefore, creates this circle we have imagined. The people who live within this circle trade across the border and, since they've been doing so for centuries, they're much closer to each other than with their own countrymen beyond the passes.

Both governments found it convenient to continue with this system after Independence, because just as it is a long way from Moreh to the nearest town in Manipur, the people of Tamu, Moreh's twin across the border are kind of cut off from the rest of the country.

Moreh today is two roads in a 'T' formation. It has been a border town since much before the British came. The road through it was used by the Burmese army during The Devastation of Seven Years. In fact, it was just the hills west of Tamu and the difficult terrain which helped the Manipur kingdom slow down the Burmese invasion back then. The road down which I have just arrived is the only link from Imphal. Moreh once used to be prosperous, particularly back in the good old days of gold and silver smuggling. The reforms ended that. Now traders bring in south Asian goods like electronic devices, cutlery of good steel, home decorations, fruits and even fabric, but one can imagine the bustle of earlier.

The axis of the T is lined with shops selling these goods, a few small and flaking restaurants, some places to stay. Mini-vans and trucks drive down the axis to a barrier about four hundred yards from the junction of the T, beyond which point vehicles are not allowed. A bus is supposed to run along these parts but that may or may not be an ancient legend.

From the barrier, goods are unloaded from the vans and carried by labourers to the Indian guard post, which is basically a shack which fits about four guards at a time and was last painted in the 1970s, from the look of things. Across a narrow passage through this shack, the labourers carry their loads over the 15 feet or so of no-man's land and through an identical shack where the Myanmar guards sit.

There are many such twin towns in the North-east. My favourite is Darranga Mela in Rangia district in Lower Assam, which looks over the border at Samdrup Dzongkhar.

If it weren't for the guards, they could be taken for a single town. It makes a great entry point into Bhutan, which is a simply awesome country which you should mark down to visit quickly because it is now a democracy so its government will publicise several awesome places so well that Joey boy might reach there before you do.

On the India-Myanmar border, though, Moreh-Tamu is my favourite. This has to do with what I call the no-man's land rule. This patch of land, true to its name, is usually a forbidding little place. There are very few border entry points where the no-man's land is kind of inviting and *meek*, that's the right word. At Moreh, it is meek, despite the problems of the lands around it. You don't feel much hesitation in crossing it.

The border closes at three in the afternoon every day, by which time people have to return to their respective countries unless they can make suitable . . . shall we say, arrangements for the night.

People who travel from Imphal or elsewhere for work in Tamu, therefore, stay at these small lodges at Moreh for the night. The price is reasonable but they won't get you food unless you agree to share the dinner the caretakers make for themselves. Before I fix things for the last leg of this run, I get lunch at a small and cramped restaurant. It is hill-river fish curry plus that smelly soup which has hounded me from Imphal. Man, I wish the people here ate something else for a change. But the curry itself is nicely done, if a bit spicy.

Saidul, the driver of my van, has been a great companion on the ride, with a lot of politically incorrect and, I suspect, very privately-held remarks about the state of things in Manipur. He has also, somehow, taken it upon himself to play host to me in Moreh, doubtless impressed by my travelling alone for no particular reason that he can understand. So I stay for the night at this place he partly owns, where between him, Arun the caretaker boy and me, we make this nice dinner which is only slightly affected by the fact that Arun, being a somewhat devout Vaishnavite Meitei, will only eat fish, Saidul can't touch pork and I have had enough of fish soup for like three lifetimes and miss pork something bad.

Towards the late afternoon, after the border closes for the day and the mini-trucks leave for the rest of Manipur, Arun's neighbours drop in. They are mostly Tamils. There are many Tamils and Muslims in Moreh. The Tamils, like their compatriots across the border, are the remains from translocations during the Raj. Most of their grandfathers and such worked on plantations and in mines deep in Myanmar, till the war pushed them to Manipur, where they settled down with some of their relations who had already been in the area for a long while. Back in 1995, when ethnic tensions erupted between them and the Kuki tribe, more than 80 per cent of them left for south India.

Kukis are found in several parts of the North-east: Karbi Anglong in Assam, Nagaland, Manipur and elsewhere, and are related to the Mizos. Unfortunately–for them–Kukis are not in a majority in any part of the region. They have thus been on the receiving end of some vicious clashes down the years. Today they have several insurgent groups such as the Kuki Liberation Front (KLF) and Kuki National Volunteers (KNV), but these are dwarfed by the groups of larger people, so they kind of try to make do.

Kukis are distinctive in appearance–swarthy and generally thin-structured. One of my co-passengers in the van is a Kuki woman who gave birth to a baby the previous night in Imphal and is carrying it back home. The husband did not go with her to the hospital. Saidul says Kukis are just like that, stoic and somewhat insensitive. I have met quite a few Kukis who are not, but Saidul, as I said, has his own way of expressing things.

So, back in the mid-Nineties, the Kukis of this area rose up in a big way and took to militancy, like the rest of Manipur. One moment they were living next to Tamils, the next they abducted some of them and threatened the others with all kinds of horrific consequences if they didn't leave, so they left.

Arun's friend Murugan was just a small boy back then, so he remembers with great clarity the sudden changes in the wind. His uncle was abducted and kept by the Kukis for a while and tortured for some extortion money. They paid but didn't move away. Just at that moment, as he is telling me the story, his uncle walks across the street from the hotel's door where we sit on *murhas*. He calls his uncle across and the man lifts up his vest to show a deep line of multiple scars running across his stomach, distinctive machete marks.

There are many other stories of translocation, ethnic strife and discord and striving from these parts that the locals tell me. And then, in the late afternoon, Arun and Murugan join two other Tamil boys for a scratch game of sepak takraw on the now-empty street. These three obvious Tamils and this one obvious Meitei, they play without nets or the usual five-a-side teams, but they are good at keeping the ball up.

Sepak takraw is one of those games, you know, easy to learn, very hard to master. For those not acquainted with it: the ball is made of bent cane or thin bamboo splits, rolled up. The teams have to serve with their hands and return using their elbows, knees and heads. Man, that ball is *hard*, okay? Manipur is good at it. Countries like Thailand and Malaysia are the powerhouses here. I could make a remark on this sight about sports uniting people and such, but I'd rather tell you about where I go next. One of the people at the *murha* meeting is this Muslim uncle, who then proceeds to tell me all about the Muslims of Tamu. There are quite a few here, and I meet the local mullah, who invites me to the roof of his house, from where I get a great photograph of what he says is the tallest minaret in Manipur, across the street. He says to get the photograph, quick, before the sun goes down, and is happy I get a good pic. The cam saves me blushes again. Man, carrying a cam like that around can be a big responsibility because everyone assumes you're a professional at it.

At night, after dinner, I lie up to get a sneak shot of Kuki militants who come into town and the border patrols who do not bother them and have a thing going in heroin with them. When I hear this story I say, golly, I can catch them right at it if I play it smart. But it is not my lucky evening. It is just the border patrols walking around.

Kuki militants, not having a large mass base to get taxes from, were among the earliest to take to drug smuggling. Most Manipur militants do it, but the Kukis got there first and today have like no-aggression pacts with everyone, so they all profit.

I sleep under the stars on the terrace of the hotel, and

try to get shots of the night sky. It is a sky worth sleeping under. The distant sounds of some theatre plus festival, where, Saidul says, the voices of the boy (*nupa*) and the girl (*nupi*) are made by the same dude, come across the night sky. The play lasts into the dawn. So do the nearer sounds of mosquitoes.

I have to make plans for the crossing. I have kept my promise not to do anything illegal, not even peek through a border fence. I go to the checkpost, where the Manipur police are polite and the Myanmarese needlessly uncivil. I try to convince the latter to permit my camera in, but they refuse. My budget does not permit the required bribe.

Myanmarese are paranoid about three things: cellphones, voice recorders and cameras. One of these days, I shall test my theory by taking half-a-kilo of good C4 or Semtex and an old Nokia across the border. I am sure they will send me back because of the Nokia. The cyclone and its aftermath have made them even more jumpy, I am told. Their government has refused aid but student groups claim large parts of the country are suffering appalling conditions because of this. Foreign media has not been permitted into these parts.

The north has not been affected by the cyclone, but I guess these chaps have been told to specially watch out for any kind of recordings. I give up and regret being so law-abiding. Ordinarily, a few words in the right places would give the visitor a lot of leeway.

Why? This is because for more than a decade-and-a-half, Manipuri extremist groups have used this region as a safe haven. North Myanmar is notionally under Yangon or wherever they have their capital these days, but they have such a robust insurgency in these parts that some Myanmarese groups make the Tamil Eelam guys look like boy scouts.

North Myanmar has two major ethnic groups: Kachin and Karen, which have never got along with the people of the Irrawaddy. Another group in Myanmar is the Shan people, who are ethnic cousins of the Ahoms. The people of the Irawaddy down south conquered these parts in the nineteenth century, but rebels have been active in the hard mountains and valleys and passes, fighting running battles with the junta.

The Kachins have been particularly good at this. In fact, they've managed to drive out the junta's soldiers, so there are large parts of northern Myanmar where the soldiers, or even local administration, can't enter without the Kachins' provisional government's permission. Of course, Yangon keeps denying that any such reversal has ever taken place. I suspect after Colombo defeated the LTTE, the junta is even more embarrassed of admitting it, but here's the truth, 'cause I know: up in the north, the junta's troops don't mess with the Kachins.

Incid., if you're ever there in the jungles of northern Myanmar, do be careful about not falling sick. That's like an even bigger concern than getting a lead injection, as they say colloquially. Y'see, these forests are so thick and swampy and such, they're full of all manner of diseases best left alone. Back in the 14th, the Mongols invaded and took northern Burma. What they brought back from the remote forests here, however, included the bubonic plague, which had kept away from mankind because *no one came to these forests*. The Mongols started dropping like flies, and, at the siege of the Crimean port city of Caffa in 1347, they mongolically decided to sic the mankiller on their enemies by catapulting their plague dead over the walls. From Caffa it spread to the rest of Europe, wiping out about 60 per cent of their people, became known as the Black Death, and *kept returning.*

So, yeah, get disinfectants and keep mosquitoes and such away while there.

For decades, the northern Myanmarese rebel groups and the Arakan Liberation boys have had mostly easy alliances with the NSCN–both factions–and the ULFA, the three biggest groups in the North-east. In some cases these are alliances born of tactical necessity. In some others, the reasons are deeper. For instance, the NSCN (Khaplang) mostly consists of Konyak Nagas. There are large communities of indigenous Konyaks in north Myanmar. Ergo, they are all in it together.

I remember when we were young, the army used to arrest or shoot 'Kachin-trained militants' of the ULFA. North-eastern groups used to train en masse in the hills of Kachin, and some of the ULFA's best op-c.o.s were or are Kachin-trained and some of them, even today, are based out of there.

Karens are a different story. Like a true bully, the junta, having faced down the Kachins and finding that these people didn't blink, has, particularly in the recent past, turned its ruthlessness against the Karens. Back during the Raj, the Karens became Christians and were not much a part of mainstream Myanmarese society. After like a hundred and twenty years or so of falling within Myanmar's borders, they sort of figured they could go their own way after Independence, which, I've been told, is what democrats like Aung San had agreed on back then. But of course after he died and democracy got toasted, the junta went after these impudent people with a vengeance. Ever since Independence, the Myanmar army has hunted down and killed hundreds of thousands of Karens, who live mainly in the north-east of that country. Karen land is also mineral- and oil-rich, so that's another incentive for Myanmar to keep it. Man, that is a very difficult place to be in. I was reading this scholarly article the other day, you know the kind of piece by PhDs on international relations, and the writer said something to the effect of the situation there being the longest-running civil war in the world. No such thing, man. It is the longest-running genocide in the world: it's been on since 1948.

So you're saying, but what about the Myanmarese being Buddhist and all. You know, I despair about organised religion all the time, because it has never made the slightest difference to the way a people are. Like every other ideology or system, religion is conveniently set aside at the first moment for whatever a country or a society thinks necessary. Or worse, religion becomes a convenient excuse, and we know *that* part very well.

Buddhism, imho, is just as sensible theoretically as Christianity or Vedic Hinduism or anything else, but Buddhist countries have been just as messed up as places with any of the Abrahamic or Indian religions. If any of you journalists in the crowd here were in Sri Lanka over the last months of their civil war you'd have seen how the Buddhist monks and all encourage their army to go after the LTTE. Got no views either way, if you ask me, but still, it's kind of undignified how the monks went after Tamil blood, seeing as everything they stand for says to be kind and merciful and all.

Now, you'll say: 'But Cid, what about the video footage of all those monks at Yangon protesting for the return of democracy, and getting cracked upside the head on their marches every other day by the police just for the heck of it? Surely there is more to it!!"

Yes, surely there is (beside the rather small fact that you've cleverly made me use the last two of the few exclamation marks I had rationed for this *entire* story, dash it). Sure, most monks down south in the real Myanmar are all for democracy and equality and all, except maybe the very few who are on the junta's payroll and are, by inference, well-fed.

However, like most people in southern Myanmar, for the average monk, their definition of Myanmarese stops round about the place I am at, or perhaps not even this far north, maybe only till Rakhine province where they have that bird sanctuary everyone keeps talking about. If you were, on the remote chance, to meet a monk from the Irrawaddy basin and ask him: 'Then, sir, if democracy returns, it means referendum for the northern tribes, like Aung San promised during Independence, doesn't it? I mean, that's what democracy is, isn't it?' To which he will roll his shoulders and shrug the typical southern Myanmarese shrug you'll never forget because it's creepy, man, and he'll say: 'But why would there be a referendum? When we have democracy the northern people will stay with us, of course.'

Why, indeed, should there be a referendum, because for

that there monk, democracy would mean the southern Myanmarese civilians running the country instead of the southern Myanmarese soldiers, a sort of expanded junta. Explain *that* to the tribes who are still awaiting the Second Coming of Aung San or some such because I doubt his daughter, if'n she gets a chance, will be bold enough to dis the monks or her partymen.

Man, that's national politics right there for you. Did someone just whisper The Old Oligarch, back there? Or did I hear someone say Xenophon? No? Alright. Your conclusions. Up to you. Me, I just present the facts.

Ed.: Wha..??! Excuse me? What exactly is going on?

In short, being a Buddhist-majority country doesn't stop you from being mean, and any protest against the rape of the northern mountains is more the exception than the rule. But what, you will ask, about the large and (or so I keep hearing) vibrant democracy to the west of such a country? Why does all this never come out?

Because, of course, India is bothered about the militants from either side co-operating with one another, and lets whatever is happening in the Myanmarese north slide. In fact, I guess our policy mandarins turn cartwheels and sing hymns if the junta pays attention to our own militancy problem or suggests co-operation of any kind. Considering we have such a huge border with them, and so many militant groups from here have camps on that side, there have been very few combined operations by the two armies, and what with the Kachins being so strong these days, there might not be many in the near future. In 1994, though, the Indian and Myanmarese armies launched a pincer-op, code-named Operation Bluebird, along both sides of the Nagaland border, taking out many rebel camps. Now the action has shifted southward to where I stand, after Manipuri UGs emerged in a big way. The leaders of many Manipuri UGs live in or visit the Tamu region.

Over the years, some rules have been put into place here, as I guess in all isolated border areas in troubled times. Because these are ancient trading outposts and both regions depend on each other, the people do not require visas to cross. A visa is an inconvenience when you have to drop down to Tamu for, say, lunch. I exaggerate, but there is a deal of mobility here.

Manipur cops are alright with anything, really. Especially when I tell them where I come from and how. The Myanmarese however, specialise in glowering, because of my obvious outsider look. They also frisk me as I enter, but after a few goings and comings they do not do that. There are some chinks in the way they frisk, that I shall not mention here. Curiously, they really do not look at the identification I offer them. No passports required either. The first hundred metres beyond the Myanmar checkpoint consist of makeshift stalls selling trinkets, cutlery of good steel, the odd tin-shed clothes store or blanket-shop, and stalls where local women sell barley-and-bread dipped in a cold drink of sorts. These are popular in the sweltering heat which is a constant after the last ten kilometers down the hills. Since there has also been no rain here for a long time, the roads on both sides are dusty and the humidity makes everyone sweat.

That drink is called something-or-the-other-*phalua* which

I take to be a derivation of *faluda*. It tastes similar but the additions make it really delicious. The men wear jeans and tees like everywhere, but the women wear a sarong-blouse combination that is as true Burmese-Malay-Thai-Laotian-Vietnamese as you can get. Most women also smear a type of paste on their cheeks and foreheads: a kind of sunblock. Communication problems are compounded here. The people know excellent Manipuri, obviously, but nothing else that I know. The few words they have of Hindi are a poor substitute.

From here it is a four-kilometre walk to Tamu, or otherwise a rickshaw kind of thing or larger vans. In Tamu I take the assistance of a local cop for useful translations, a big advantage in a country where any uniform is a mark of great might. If you think police stations in India are needlessly forbidding, unfriendly or descendents of the Raj when the cop was simply a blunt instrument, you must visit Myanmar.

Each police station is barricaded and the high walls are wrapped in razor-wire. Yes, razor, not even barbed. The cops have good assault rifles and one or two of them also carry small RPGs this time (I have not seen the type before but it looks like the kid brother of a 7D). It is a good thing my local contact, U., is a cop because he says he can get most things done, and he will, too. Asking a citizen would be no use because they are all deathly scared of uniformed authority of any kind, so getting the cops to bat for you solves like all your problems. I *still* can't get my camera in but I got to be thankful for small mercies.

The shops here are busy with people from outlying hamlets and from the Indian side and many kinds of fruits and vegetables are to be found, as well as some kinds of local insects. I have a cricketish thing for lunch here with hill-river fish curry once again (practically the same as its Manipuri cousin). The c.t. is crunchy but nicely done and even comes with a separate pickle.

Perhaps this is common to all countries which try to project an image other than the truth, but it seems all border areas are neater than the rest of the country. The Wagah border is kept so spruce and impressive that one might think the rest of that country is in the contest for the Best-kept Nation Awards or something. Here, the border market has a wide road and clean buildings and everything, like they are whitewashed every Sunday. Tamu is a bit run-down but the roads are still better than on the Indian side. Beyond is a forbidding army post guarding the far pass beyond which visitors are not permitted. U. very discreetly points out the houses of some of the Manipuri militant leaders who stay here sometimes, but is very anxious to make sure I am not here to do a story on them. These are usually modest little places but very neat and newly-painted and so on, so one can imagine the kind of luxuries those guys would have inside, bought with blood money. But that is how militants live everywhere.

Drugs have replaced the silver and gold routes of earlier. Small, highly mobile and surprisingly multi-ethnic bands of smugglers travel from the river-crossed borders of Thailand and Laos through central Myanmar to Tamu and other border crossings. The first thing I noticed back when I first met one of these groups was how different communities and ethnicities, otherwise frequently in the news over some political strife with one another, cooperated in the gang. It was like they had no problems at all. There's an ironic moral right there, but it gets so twisted I don't want to talk about it just now.

The Myanmar Army and some elements of the Indian border guards are very well compensated along these routes. In fact, deep in central Myanmar, officers earn money like all the time with small processing plants where raw opium is refined into some high-grade stuff, as well as some varieties of chemical drugs, including methamphetamines which are the coming thing, mark my words. Between drugs and the other kind of trade I'm about to introduce you to, the junta has its grip on two perpetually recession-proof industries, and prospers.

Back in Moreh, I make arrangements to keep my camera at the police station (even they need convincing that I am not here to upset *their* little cross-border apple-cart). I remember that hill I had seen on the drive into town, so I walk back up to the point and climb it. It's a bit steep but uneventful and by the late afternoon I am standing on it. The view compensates.

Up another hill the following day I get what I suppose is a poor substitute for cracking sting-shots from inside Tamu–a view of the plains of Myanmar with the tin roofs of Tamu in the distance.

It is morning and the vans begin to arrive to carry the goods back. I walk across the no-entry sign and under the two flags to the post, past the Indian guards and the Myanmarese who are now practising their early-morning glares and grunts.

About a hundred yards or so down the road from the checkpoint, the shops are mostly the same as back in

Moreh, like I said, this open stall where I have the phalua, some quilt shops, some very good-quality cutlery that is much, much better than what's made in India, the usual electronics shops, things like that. Hawkers fan themselves in the early-morning heat which has just started warming up for the rest of the day (*that* was a good one), with knee-high black mounds which, on careful inspection, you will find are these tiny lockets on flimsy-looking black thread. On one side of these clear plastic lockets is the Shwedagon, looking unbelievably tacky (which is sad because that pagoda is supposed to be really nice, dunno though, never seen it) and on the other is this close-up of the chief Buddhist lama or something of Myanmar, someone whose name I had asked once or twice from people and probably remembered for a while but can't recall at the mo, but that's okay, I'll ask someone again and forget it afterwards.

If, dear frand, you decide to come down the narrow road and (my best efforts at *disinformatsia* and clueless guidance notwithstanding) you find yourself here, at the beginning of the road to Tamu, and are tempted to strike up a conversation with the little old ladies who make up most of these on-road vends, and are therefore tempted, as a sign that you-come-in-peace and all is well or some such hippy nonsense, to mark the border crossing by buying one of these lockets, man, I hereby warn you, dude, *check the currency notes.*

Y'see, Indian currency is not a problem in these parts, what with the trade and all, so you don't need to find a money-changer or somebody. But the Manipuris very cleverly take the worst of their currency notes over to Tamu and sort of pass it on whenever they get the chance, prolly to little kids and such. So eventually a rather large stream of almost-falling-apart Indian rupees lands with these here little old ladies who, being the most shrewd small businesspeople you will find on the narrow road, are the only folk willing to get rid of it. So they wait for the unwary or some numbskull from Manipur and do the reverse trick, and what are you left with? Exactly. So, insist on new notes or something.

Beyond the last of the shops off the border gate is this other gate which was put up for some strange reason I've never understood, and which is never closed. This here gate looks about a quarter size of one of the colony gates you might find all over your town, and is remarkably flimsy. And before you say a word: trust me, I know, they don't even close this gate when the border shuts, so it is totally pointless.

Well, so beyond this is a line of autorickshaw-type vehicles and a few vans for the short ride into main Tamu town. Once in town, you do your own stuff, man, I know what to do.

Because Tamu has this awesome arms bazaar which lives in the twilight zone. I know, I know, you guys are experts on arms bazaars, aren't you? You're perhaps thinking of dinky little shops in Peshawar with rifles and handguns all over the place and some bearded guy saying: 'Ekkey, ekkey?' to you, some childhood memory you've picked up from *Rambo III* because that's what you're thinking of, the dude saying : 'You fight well . . . for a *turist*.'

Na, they closed those places in Peshawar a long time ago, not that I would know anything of it. But that's not the way things are usually run. That was, shall we say, the showroom version of selling illegal weapons, a market representing the kind of culture which fires in the air at weddings or celebrations because they don't have firecrackers and after all, *bullets make a noise, don't they?*

That's the wild west. This is the matter-of-fact, professional east. No showrooms.

Firearms and such is a demand-based industry, always has been, always will be. The reason it never slumps is not because of some very cleverly-crafted marketing campaign somewhere which persuades people to buy all that metallic cargo (although gunrunners can be remarkably persuasive and slick: witness the lifestyles of some of those guys you might read about once in a while in the papers).

So, no, the firearms industry never slumps because there is always some idiot somewhere who knows exactly what he wants and tries his best to get it. Eventually, he does.

Since firearms (and let's face it, in these degenerate days very large ordnance also sells under the counter everywhere) is a specialised and technical field, these buyers know the tech-specs of the products they are looking for. Given the nature of these deals, they have to be totally on the q.t., so there are all these shady-looking fellows travelling all over the place striking bargains. Glamour is not their line: in fact, most of them go far out of their way not to be too flashy, although the dumb short-run guys show up at high-end hotels in Ras-el-Khaimah or someplace with a faux supermodel or two. So, for the pros, no showrooms. The international arms market, in the places where legitimate state-to-state purchases go off the map and touch no-state players, works on a few established supply routes, where virtually all the players are acquainted with one another, operational security and such is very tight and more things are hinted at than said.

Among the largest sellers is the US armaments industry, which sells off surplus or superannuated ordnance to private buyers, often without much oversight on the links behind them, although things have become tight in the last nine years. These buyers then funnel the arms—which are very good, if not cutting-edge—to buyers around the world. The Chinese do the same, but their quality, like that of other products from that country, sucks. It is only a desperate or dumb warlord or insurgent group which bases its ops around arms purchases from China, and since this is a direct quote from this deep source of mine, you can take that as a fact.

Another route is when an old, established military or militia group disbands. In such a scenario, the group sends out the underground equivalent of a classified ad to the effect that their stuff is up on the market and open to the highest bidder. For instance, back in 1987, the Khmer Rouge, practically on the ropes, unloaded their humungous arsenal on the South Asian market, causing numerous runners everywhere to suddenly and simultaneously start believing in all the gods they should have followed. And a large chunk of that, from what I gather the single-biggest fraction, was bought up by the ULFA, which was at the height of its operational capability, which not only shows that the outfit was like loaded with fresh extortion money, but also had a huge ambition and organisational ego back in the day. I mean, if a group says to itself that it will buy guns from the Khmer Rouge, it means the group views itself as a premier fighting force in Asia.

Of course the ULFA eventually turned out to be a joke and an embarrassment for the people of Assam, what with their random killings in the Nineties, getting kicked out of Bhutan in 2003 by the Royal Freakin' Bhutan Army and bombing little kids and what not, their big houses and businesses in Bangladesh and elsewhere and such other ridiculous stuff. Today the ULFA is, as said, a perpetual joke, in case some of you guys wanted to ask how safe Assam is. Well, it *is* safe, so you needn't worry about them boys anymore. They're old fat men and they aren't going to do anything.

Coming back to the arms industry, then, such big going-out-of-business sales are the exception rather than the norm, because these no-state groups tend to hang around till they are wiped out (re LTTE), stick around to make more money for the bosses (re ULFA) or have a dialogue thingy going for the time being (re NSCN), and therefore hang on to their guns. So the new kids need to look elsewhere for their popguns.

In the North-east, with its 103 militant groups (at current count), there is another interesting game of firearms musical chairs which has over the years evolved into a fine art. One group or sub-group surrenders to the government or the army in a publicised ceremony with all the bells and whistles. Count the number of men surrendering and the arms they give up, as well as the quality of said ws. There is almost always a mismatch. Those missing weapons and ammo (which are invariably the best the group has) are sold off to active groups at subsidised rates which go into various squirrel funds the leaders have. This money comes into use eventually when the former militants enter politics and need to fund their campaign, or when the cadre enters another business, re drugs.

Back in the day, a small bunch of Bodo militants had surrendered in west Assam, so I was asked by the paper to go take a look. I was a rookie and the senior reporters had gotten bored with that stuff a long time ago, so it wasn't like I could refuse the assignment, okay?

So there was another one of those white-clad tables on which this bunch of guns, bullets and a sorry-looking collection of grenades had been arranged rather neatly by the army. Man, none of those guns even looked safe to use, I mean they were like real antique pieces, alright. So my contact, this nice guy from MI who'd a wicked sense of humour after four years in the bush doing god-knows-what, asks me: 'You want to try blowing up your hand with one of those?'

It's like that. Happens all the time, this selling off the real guns business.

I tell you, in the last twenty years or so since the MNF in Mizoram, as I said, left fighting and came to power, every other group with a BB gun and a stick or two has like this holy grail of eventual electoral victory, and this surrender business has become a Groucho Marx movie without the funny bits and *with* like tonnes of that weird moustache all over the place. No paper or channel even covers them if the event takes place far away from the big towns, which is a dashed good idea. But who's to tell the state governments?

In Tamu, if you have a contact or two (which you won't, because you're not subterranean people, are you? Ha, ha. Erm, are you?) you'll check up with them if they've got like samples and such, which you'll check to make sure no one's gypping you, following which you fix the deal.

Alternately, not being subterranean and therefore sadly a babe in the woods (re *moi*) but possessed of enough persuasion to convince the players that there's no harm in letting you take a look at the merchandise because your views of the law (if not your usual lifestyle) match their own, you will be given a kind of grand tour, in which you might or might not see the samples or get to visit the shady little shacks where they store the rest of their stuff.

The guns you will find at Tamu are mostly first-hand or well-kept second-hands. Considering these second-hands have been out under the rains and mud and such for a while, the fact that they're in good working condition and even shiny, as I check 'em, means the people hawking them know a thing or two about maintenance, and know where to spot a good bargain wherever they source them from.

Price tags? A very good .38 revolver comes at Rs 10,000, max, maybe lower if you bargain. But there's no point because you can't bring it into India, not the way you or I will return.

The people who run this in Tamu, on a much, much smaller scale than, say, on the Thai border and other parts, the government makes sure these guns are not for their insurgents, but for other countries. Like I said, smart.

Meanwhile, as U. and I take in the delights of this wacky place, other events have been unfolding. In a dusty corner of a shop run by this ancient man of uncertain ethnic origin and highly suspect hygiene I find, under like half-a-dozen gunny sacks, a length of red. I have a rare hunch, and on looking into it I unearth a factory-made *bushi dai-katana* with this simply delightfully crafted black metal hilt-guard (called a *tsuba*) and red enamelled wooden scabbard.

This single find makes the Cid's entire week, because there is no way I can leave it behind. We eventually coax out of the ancient one that the dai-katana must have been part of a cargo of display swords he had got into Tamu from Thailand sometime in the past, possibly with the intent of sending them off into Manipur at vastly inflated prices to con someone or the other. By the look of things, while stored at this decrepit shop, the best of the lot must have slipped out and fallen into difficult circumstances. Having rescued it, I am now determined to bring it back with me. Also in that there shop I find a set of a smaller katana, called, I believe, a *wakizashi*, and a *tanto*, which is like a small dagger. The hilts on these two are made of carved dragons and on the tips of their scabbards, man, there are these gnome-like faces on them. Can't leave them behind.

By this time the ancient one has bestirred himself with joy and shows me a Thai ceremonial dagger which I also grab, before U. takes me out into the sobering light of the day and on to other delights of Tamu town.

Which reminds me: everyone in Moreh, on the India side, is armed, okay, although not with guns. Back when I was talking with Arun and Murugan at the hotel, a friend of theirs came down the street, said hello to me, and pulled out this *big* army knife, which on closer examination turned out to be Thai-made, you know, one of those things which says 'USA Saber' in glazed green on the hilt. A very good quality piece made of excellent steel that was, too, the blade about a foot long and the price of Rs 200 sent other people to the place he had bought it off.

So now you'll ask me: 'But Cid, having bought these admittedly nice-looking pieces and having succeeded in convincing us that you, as we suspected, are a certifiable nut, how will you now bring them back to your base, namely, Delhi? Assuming, that is, you do not wish to donate them somewhere.'

Good question. Y'see, here's the best part about crossing into Myanmar. They don't like you going in, and they make no bones about it, but so long as you mind your business and don't make an ass of yourself and know the ins and outs, they won't bother you. They won't let you take in cellphones and cameras, but *they really don't care what you bring back.*

They really don't. You can load yourself in bushi armour and return on horseback waving two swords if you like, they will continue sitting on their murhas and yawning.

The problem is on the Indian side, where the cops and what-not check what you're bringing back, but once you've told them it's harmless and you aren't going to destabilise Manipur and besides, tell them you've been on the road all these days and won't stand for nonsense, they back off. But you have to keep doing this at each checkpoint, and make sure you walk with the car as they check it, or they'll break some of your purchases just to be obnoxious. But so far as swords go, it's easy.

After Manipur there are no checks till Guwahati airport (or Imphal if you want the fast extraction route), where you can have a word or two with the security officer of your airline and sort things out.

And *that* is also how people bring in drugs from Tamu, except every checkpoint has a fixed quota of bribes, proportionate to quantity of shipment, as I've been told, and they don't risk flying afterwards.

After seeing the usual eyesores at Tamu and listening to U., who is also a poet, talk about the birds of Victoria Peak down in Rakhine province, where he is from, we continue up the road east to the mountain pass guarded by the Myanmar Army, beyond which travel is not allowed without a visa (do I need to say 'official travel'?). Here I have a blood-curdlingly bad glass of tea with the captain in charge of the unit, who wants to know all about Delhi and scowls a great deal on hearing I'm a journalist. He takes a while to be convinced that journalising is definitely not what I'm here to do and even cracks a trace of a smile on hearing about the *katana*. There is a lot of back-and-forth in their tongue between U. and him before it finally dawns on him that I am not going to return that afternoon at 3 pm, but by the end of the hour, on hearing about other journeys I have had thereabouts, he is okay.

God, I don't know if he's ever been posted in Kachin or Karen land or how many democrat heads he's busted. He does his job, as do his men. What are these people, anyway? Are they, because they serve an unquestionably evil regime and follow orders, themselves evil, or are they just people being, you know, people?

I am standing on a hill off the road to Tamu and the valley is beneath. I shall be doing a lot of walking in these parts, looking into various matters. The heat is less up here and a wind of some kind is blowing.

I sit on an overhang and think of this and that. Cliff overhangs, I have discovered, are an excellent place to sit and think of random stuff. Must have something to do with the view. I can see most of Tamu and all of Moreh from here and, inside, I see the rest of the narrow road stretching from where it began till this place. It is as good a place as any to take stock.

Somebody has expressed the hope that I shall find myself on this trip. It is a nice wish, but I think the necessity of finding oneself only emerges when one loses oneself, *n'est-ce pas?* And *that* would really worry me ... It is true that to travel is to 'drink life to the lees', but remember the man who wrote this never went beyond Birmingham. It is all a function of how much one gains from the different endeavours one begins, be it travel or writing codes for a software firm or building bridges. Or how one chooses to finish these endeavours. And even that depends on how one defines gain. But I agree with the chap when he says 'all experience is an arch wherethro' ...' etc. (Hey, don't bug me about who I quote, okay, I'll think of someone more recent the next time). It's been nice coming up here with you guys, great sharing the narrow road east of the sun. I guess you will have to turn back from here. I'll go ahead and take a look around. I mean, there'll *always* be something new to add to the bag. Bye.

P.S. Oh, certainly, ma'am. If I find any more interesting stuff I'll tell you guys everything about it. Which reminds me, man, I got to tell you, this one time ...

Ed.: Another story? Does this mean *another* story? Another time, then?

9 789380 658360